The Splendour of Antique Rugs and Tapestries

The Splendour of Antique Rugs and Tapestries

Parviz Nemati

ANTIQUE COLLECTORS' CLUB

pdn
communications

Cover: Detail from 19th century Ushak carpet
Photo: Don Tuttle

Back Cover: Detail from 18th century Brussels tapestry
Photo: Hossein Montazaran

End Paper: Detail from 16th century alcaraz carpet
Photo: Hossein Montazaran

First published 2001
© Parviz Nemati 2001
World copyright reserved

PDN Communications
Antique Collectors' Club, Woodbridge ISBN 1 85149 381 6

British Library Cataloguing-in-Publication Data
A catalogue record for this book is available from the British Library

Published in the United Kingdom by the Antique Collectors' Club Ltd.,
Woodbridge, Suffolk IP12 1DS

Graphic Design, printing and binding by Lannoo Printers, Tielt/Belgium
www.lannooprint.be

Acknowledgements

I have been inspired to write this book by many people and events, however there are certain people that I would like to thank in particular. The interior designers and collectors whom are an important part of my business over the years were the initial impetus for this book but they are too numerous to mention.

However I, am most indebted to my son, Darius, who manages the Nemati Collection and has greatly supported me in the preparation of this volume. His enthusiasm encouraged me to expand on the issues raised in *Rugs as an Investment* and to build on its success. In addition, the support of HALI, the foremost carpet and textile art magazine, is great importance to me. This publication has been instrumental in developing the international carpet market, and has, in its own way, made this book possible. In particular Ben Evans, Sebastian Ghandchi and Daniel Shaffer have all been of great help in the many guises of advisor, editor, expert and friend. Liz Dixon has used her extensive expertise in the field of art book publishing to design and manage the creation of this spectacular volume. I would also like to thank Mirela Mindrean and Emma Sjöstrom whose organizational skills have been invaluable to me as my personal assistants, and Laurence Khan for his constant support.

During the three years I have spent researching this book, I have come to realize that writing about rugs gives me as much pleasure and satisfaction as the rugs themselves. The antique rug business, in which I have been involved for most of my life, has provided me with the vision and opportunity to explore other areas of the world of carpets, textiles and Islamic art. I look forward to immersing myself in the world of book writing and publishing, and starting the next of these projects with great anticipation.

Table of Contents

Foreword

I am delighted to have been asked to contribute a foreword to Parviz Nemati's long-awaited second book on oriental rugs and tapestries. The earlier volume, the best-selling *Rugs as an Investment,* was published in 1980, and immediately established an international reputation for the Iranian born, American educated, Mr. Nemati, who was by then already one of the youngest of New York City's leading dealers in antique oriental rugs, with an elegant gallery in the design district.

It has taken a full generation of experience and achievement at the sharp end of the carpet market for Parviz to realize this successor volume. As one would expect, in its scope and content the book reflects the enormous growth and change in this fascinating and adventure-filled market. In his introduction, Parviz observes that over the course of the second half of a forty-year career immersed in oriental rugs, the emphasis in the market has changed. In New York today, the investment value of fine carpets and rugs, the key factor in many buying choices a quarter of a century ago, has become of less consequence, with decorative qualities the driving force instead.

The book has at its heart a collection of some three hundred carefully chosen antique rugs, carpets, kilims and tapestries, both Oriental and European – this latter an essential addition to the fashionable New York gallery's repertoire. Although just a representative selection from the thousands of carpets, rugs and tapestries Parviz has owned and handled over the years, almost all are of types that are both available and affordable. In their quality and diversity they reflect the innate taste, style and thoughtful learning of their owner. For Parviz has always been a connoisseur and educator as well as a dealer, with an interest and involvement in the weaver's art that goes far beyond the simply commercial, and owes so much to his fondly-remembered childhood in the South Persian city of Kerman.

Two or three years ago, at their gallery in New York, Parviz talked to me of his 'imminent' plans for retirement and relaxation with his family. However, he also admits that rugs are in the blood as long as we all live and breathe.

Daniel Shaffer
Editor, HALI

Introduction

There are certain sights and sounds I remember vividly from my childhood in the Iranian rug-weaving center of Kerman. Dark, wet, freshly dyed wool drying on neighboring rooftops was as familiar a part of the landscape as the mountains encircling the arid plains of my home. I can still see the shady rooms with dirt floors where young girls, known as *bafandeh*, worked steadily, fingers flying as they tied the knots of what became exquisite rugs. As they worked, the girls counted the knots through chanting, and I often woke to this rhythmic sound in the early morning, when the air was still cool and the light fresh. These memories are still fresh decades later.

Before the late 19th century, the designs of oriental rugs and the particular style of each rug-weaving area reflected distinct cultural and historical influences which had remained uninterrupted for thousands of years. This remarkable legacy provided an enormous language of naturalistic and geometric motifs and color harmonies. The weavers who made these rugs learnt from early childhood the grammar and vocabulary of their village or regional traditions; with their mastery of weaving came the almost poetic ability to incorporate into the traditional designs personal interpretations of deeply held spiritual beliefs. This long tradition, although conservative, also provided the secure framework from which the weavers gained the freedom to improvise and impart into every rug a unique character and composition, a feature much admired today.

Since the publication of my last book, *Rugs as an Investment* (Agate Press, New York, 1980), major changes have reshaped and expanded the international market of this art form. This has resulted in more emphasis being placed on the decorative aspects of rugs and tapestries with investment becoming a secondary consideration.

There has been a huge increase in the amount of books and periodicals on the subject of antique rugs and tapestries, and several important private collections have been formed such as the Orient Stars collection of Heinrich Kirchheim (*Orient Stars*, E. Heinrich Kirchheim et al., Stuttgart 1993) as well as important exhibitions hosted by major museums like 'Flowers Under Foot - Indian Carpets from the Mughal Era' (November 1997 - March 1998) at the Metropolitan Museum Of Art in New York.

HALI, the magazine of carpet, textile and Islamic art, has become the most authoritative and finely designed publication for studies of this form of art. Major rug and textile collections have been successfully sold at auction, such as those of Bernheimer, Dildarian, Mayorcas, Vigo-Sternberg, and Yves Mikaeloff. Huge prices have been achieved by these sales, the Bernheimer sale of rugs and textiles in 1996 brought over $4 million and in 1999, four carpets from the Rothschilds of Vienna, Austria made over $22.5 million. These prices show that there is a lot of competition from around the world for the best rugs and tapestries on the market.

Cyberspace and the information super-highways of the new millennium might be very fascinating to many people, but the appreciation of art will remain a constant comfort to the human soul; the charm and beauty of woven art in the form of rugs and tapestries will continue to mesmerize people for the foreseeable future. The art of rug and tapestry weaving has been in existence for millennia, and if the future brings cloned sheep and robot weavers, the distinct nature and creations of this art, formed through intertwining human creativity and ingenuity, will continue to delight the human senses.

This book is the result of forty years of passion for the woven art. Having spent much of my life with artists, designers, collectors, dealers, and historians of woven art, I have always felt the need for a book that focuses the attention of all interested parties and takes them on a journey through the wonderful world of rugs and tapestries. In writing this book, I have tried to combine information and illustration. Importantly, the rugs and tapestries described are still available in today's market, they are affordable and functional. Indeed, in this field, form and function – or pleasure and use – can hardly be separated. These rugs and tapestries were made to have practical as well as decorative functions: tapestries illustrate important people and historic events and were used to stop the cold in castles and churches; rugs were to be walked upon, sat upon, lived upon. Rugs and tapestries do and have always displayed wealth and status. Like many objects of intrinsic quality, they improve with age as colors mature, fibers soften and the patina develops from use and age. Some say that this is the rug's or tapestry's soul and is the gift of the weaver's hand and eye. It becomes apparent along with the more tangible aspects.

I begin with a brief history of rugs, followed by a discussion of the techniques of rug making and then I survey the major rug-producing areas. The rugs, which are also described in detailed captions, date primarily from the 19th and 20th centuries and are from Persia (Iran), Turkey, the Caucasus, Turkestan, India and China. A major addition to the previous book is the inclusion of rugs and tapestries from Europe, most notably France, Spain and England. The tapestries date from the early 16th century and come from Northern Europe.

Since I am trying to cover rugs and tapestries of the world in one volume, I have judged that the aim of the technical and historical information, diagrams and maps should be to furnish designers, architects, dealers and collectors with satisfactory information whilst making the book accessible and digestible to a wider audience. Throughout the book I have maintained a practical and pragmatic viewpoint.

How could it be otherwise? I grew up with rugs and have devoted my adult life to studying, buying and selling them. By writing on this subject, I am trying to share my knowledge and enthusiasm with my readers.

A History of Rug Making

The patterns and techniques used in making knotted rugs have been used for millennia, however their origins are uncertain. Pile weavings may have developed to imitate animal skins by early nomads or made in an urban environment to replace and mimic floor mosaics. Many authors, including Kurt Erdmann in *Seven Hundred Years Of Oriental Carpets*, (London, 1970), believe the art to have originated in East Turkestan, where sheep-herding nomads made rugs to insulate themselves and cover floors bedding in their tents which were easy to transport.

Only a small number of early rugs have been preserved and are now in museum and private collections. The fact that the materials used are of a perishable nature and that the objects were often heavily used means textiles and rugs are less likely to survive than many other objects. What survives must be considered to be a fraction of what once existed.

We owe a debt of gratitude to the preservative quality of the Siberian ice at Pazyryk in the Altai Mountains in Mongolia for preserving the earliest knotted rug. In 1949 a team of Soviet archaeologists discovered the Pazyryk carpet in a Scythian burial mound. Although it has since been radiocarbon-14 dated to the 4-5th century BC, the brilliant red and green tones continue to glow. The carpet has a central field of tile-like motifs surrounded by multiple borders which depict broad-antlered spotted deer, carefully drawn uniformed horsemen, and griffins amongst other things. Recent research and discoveries seem to point to a Central Asian origin for the carpet, however whatever the provenance of the carpet may be, it is clear that the carpet is a product of an established and remarkably sophisticated rug-weaving culture.

As early as the eighth century B.C., sources from Egypt, Greece, Phoenicia, Mesopotamia, and Persia tell us that wealthy families frequently adorned their palaces with magnificent rugs, and that the production of rugs was based on a highly sophisticated industry. Epics from Shahnameh's *The Book of Kings* recount how the floors of the palace of Harun ar-Rashid displayed some 22,000 rugs woven in Khorasan. Perhaps the most valuable Persian rug ever woven was the *Spring of Khosrow* Carpet from the sixth century. The colossal rug (purported to measure about 11,300 square feet) was woven in silk, embroidered with gold and silver, and encrusted with jewels. It inspired the homage of poets and enlivened the palace of Khosrow I at Ctesiphon, but it was eventually hacked to pieces by the soldiers of the Muslim army.

Apart from examples of loop pile textiles attributed to the Copts of the earlier Christian era in Egypt, chronologically the next surviving carpets are made during the period of the Seljuk Empire (960-1243) which incorporated Asia Minor, Persia, Mesopitamia and Syria. In 1272 Marco Polo mentioned carpets from this area being the finest in the world. Some fragments of carpets from this period were found in the early 20 century in the great Mosque of Ala-ad-Din in Konya, Central Turkey.

Early Ottoman Weaving

The area now occupied by Turkey is an area that has been occupied by Hittites, Scythians, Greeks, Romans, Medes, Byzantines, Seljuk Turks, Mongols, the Crusaders and, eventually, the Osmani or Ottoman Turks. In the 14th century the Ottomans were developing their empire and their own court style. The earliest carpets known from this period are the dragon and phoenix carpets. One of these rugs is in the Islamisches Museum in Berlin, Germany and this type is seen in some 15th century Italian paintings.

The old carpet traditions of the displaced Seljuks and the Mamluks of Egypt and Syria, which were brought into the Ottoman Empire in 1517, were absorbed and developed into an Ottoman style. Rugs and textiles with geometric repeat designs employing stars, octagons, squares, and triangles were woven in cherry red, yellow-green, and pale blues. The Ottoman court style came to favor more floral curvilinear elements rather than focusing on the geometric designs of the cultures it had absorbed (plate 1). This change in style has been related to the Ottoman capture of the Safavid capital Tabriz in 1514 and the influence of the captured Safavid art and artists.

Four main types of Ottoman rugs from the 14th and 15th centuries are shown in European paintings of the time in which they are used as symbols of status. Two of these carpet types have been named after the painters in whose paintings they appear, Lorenzo Lotto and Hans Holbein.

The rugs of the Ottoman Empire were exported into Europe in large numbers and by the 16th century, the Sultan's workshops had evolved a unique style which remained popular into the 20th century. One important aspect of this production was that of fine prayer rugs in centers such as Ghiordes, Ladik, Melas, Kula and Konya. These prayer rugs are found in relatively large numbers throughout the West and constitute a great proportion of the early museum collections formed at the beginning of 20th century.

The special relationship which emerged in the 18th century between the Ottoman Sultans and the French Kings led to an artistic exchange between the two nations. The French Savonnerie incorporated Turkish bird and flower designs, and Turkish weavers adapted French floral and coats of arms motifs (plate 155). The French influence was most pronounced under the Sultan Abdul Mejid, a francophile known as 'Monsieur Osman.' At his newly established looms in Hereke, he initiated the *mejid* Ghiordes style famed for its pink rose designs on a rich pistachio background.

The court art and grand artistic patronage of the 16th and 17th centuries produced designs and fashions which trickled down to the lower echelons of Ottoman society. The influence and style of the early Ottoman period can be seen in the weavings made in the 18th and 19th century and even today (plate 156).

Persian Carpets

One of the greatest periods of creativity in the art of the rug weaving took place in Persia during the rule of the Safavid dynasty (1499-1722). The beauty of Persian court art in the 16th and 17th centuries influenced the Indian Mughal Empire which in turn produced their own Persian style carpets at the height of their empire's wealth.

In Persia during the reigns of Shah Tahmasp (1524-1576) and Shah Abbas (1588-1629) weaving became an established large-scale artistic and commercial enterprise revolving around highly skilled and organized weaving workshops. The designs of rugs became curvilinear rather than rectilinear and what had essentially been a cottage industry became court art. This rich artistic climate was enjoyed by miniature painters, calligraphers, philosophers, mathematicians and weavers alike; all artisans worked in harmony under royal patronage and developed a style which had distinct universal characteristics. Court painters designed complex curvilinear floral patterns which decorated book covers and these were interpreted into cartoons for use in carpets (plate 2).

Some of these carpets incorporate wool, silk, silver and gold-thread in their complex woven structures. One of the more famous groups of these carpets is the so-called Polonaise carpet which, believed to have been made in Isfahan, have survived in a many European public and private collections.

plate **1** | Ottoman Cairene
Late 16th century
11'7" x 19' (3.53 x 5.79m)
*This rug illustrates the union of
two distinct artistic traditions
that flourished under two of the
most powerful Islamic dynasties
of the 15th and 16th centuries,
namely the Mamluk Sultanate
and the Ottoman Empire. The
present rug belongs to a well-
known and documented group of
rugs, which display the technical
characteristics of Mamluk
weaving traditions as well as the
decorative style and
ornamentation of the Ottoman
Court workshops. The graceful,
elaborate floral patterns of these
carpets were most likely
introduced to the Egyptian looms
with the Ottoman conquest of
the Mamluk Empire in 1517.
What really sets this rug apart is
that many of the design elements
utilized are not available in the
19th and 20th century rugs
found readily in the market.
Furthermore, the effects of time
and wear have produced some
unique colors that exude
elegance. From the center star
radiates a series of elaborate
stemmed flowers and leafy plants
in a time-worn hunter green
color also found in some of the
large scale encased flower motifs
of the field. The soft shades of
velvet red and pen ink blue clue
us to the bold colors the rug must
have had when woven.
The border design of very large
palmettes and serrated fig leaves
are framed by a guard border
design reminiscent of a chess-set
Rook.*

History

plate **2** | 17TH CENTURY SILK
3'10" x 6'5" (1.17 x 1.96m)
*17th century Silk with
debatable origin, attributed to
Persia or Turkey.*

The best-recorded examples of the Polanaise carpets are the eight pieces in the Redens Museum in Munich, Germany which were part of the dowry of the Polish Princess Anna Kathrin Konstanza when she married Elector Palatine Philip Wilhem in 1642. The rich colors and glittering surface of the silk and metal thread grounds mesmerized the European courts. It is thought that these particular pieces were given as diplomat gifts.

The cities of Tabriz, Kashan, Herat and Kerman evolved into busy centers of production. The royal looms of Shah Abbas at Isfahan also worked for the early export trade. Large carpets showing the Garden and Vase designs and elegant prayer rugs were among their output coveted abroad (plates 100, 101, 119, 121, 123).

The beauty and sophistication of the Safavid period rugs can only be rivaled by the achievements of the book illumination and calligraphy of the period. The characteristics of the Safavid style can be seen in equal measure in all of these disciplines and these arts laid the foundations of the Persian weaving tradition. This inheritance can be seen in the Northwest Persia carpet (plate 4): its lobed central medallion laid on its all over floral field pattern is derived from the Safavid medallion tradition.

 The 18th century signaled a time of political instability in Persia and few court commissions led to the demise of the court manufactories and the displacement of large sections of the population. Thus, the inspiration and impetus responsible for such masterpieces as the 16th century Ardebil Carpets, in the Victoria and Albert Museum in London and the Los Angeles County Museum, was lost.

Little is known about 18th century Persian rugs, although occasionally, some beautiful examples can be found (plate 4). Alongside the metropolitan tradition, a rural or more localized production was established, continued today in ethnic groups such as the Kurds, Afshars, and Qashqa'i.

A Persian weaving revival occurred during the second half of the 19th century, through more economic stability and the growth of demand for carpets throughout the West, especially in the USA. These rugs established a tradition which is still visible today, exhibiting a bridge from the past to the future. The free artistic expression found in tribal weavings synthesizes the Safavid inheritance and local tribal emblems; workshop carpets continue the formal repertoire established by court workshops.

Early Indian Weaving

The establishment of the Mughul dynasty in India in the early 16th century produced a sudden period of remarkable advances and growth in Indian rug making. Akbar (1556-1605), the grandson of Babur the founder of the Mughul dynasty, transformed what was a small indigenous industry weaving coarse rugs into one existing within the context of court workshops. Akbar installed major court looms in Northwestern India and imported book designers and illuminators of manuscripts from Persia whose designs set the style for all the allied arts. The patronage of Akbar and the popularity of the Persian designs explain why many Indian rugs following seem similar to Persian models. From the late 17th century onwards a distinct Mughul style developed that has particular colors and motifs – realistic depiction of flowers and shrubs and lattices are particular favorites of the Mughul repertoire.

The large workshops set up by the Mughuls at Agra, Lahore, Amritsar and Kashmir continue to produce carpets up to the present day. The British expanded production by putting prisoners to work. The prison workshops of the 19th century produced many fine rugs which trace their designs back to the early Mughul period.

Early Chinese Weaving

In China carpet making was not an established part of court art as it was in the neighboring Islamic countries. Not until the establishment of the Manchu dynasty in the mid 17th century, which had roots in nomadism, is there any evidence of carpet making. However in East Turkestan, Tibet and Mongolia, all areas that the Han Chinese see as ethnic minority provinces, a long history of rug weaving and use does exist.

Although current research has established a dating for a small group of carpets to the Ming period (prior to 1644), the earliest records referring to rug production in mainland China date from the reign of Emperor H'ang His (1662-1722). The Emperor invited Chinese painters in Peking to make rug designs, and sent abroad for foreign master weavers. The rugs were design to be used as covers for chairs, saddles, pillars throne daises and floors alike. The height of rug weaving came during Ch'ien Lung's reign (1736-1796). The production was established in workshops in and around Ningxia. These remained productive into the twentieth century, Chinese rugs continued to be made with thick pile and simple color variations, embodying a rich language of symbols.

Most early Chinese rugs were produced in the Northern and Western provinces adjoining Mongolia, East Turkestan, and Tibet which is the area associated with wool production in China. The indigenous weaving tradition of East Turkestan is distinguished by the people's Turkic origins. The oasis cities of Khotan, Yarkand, and Kashgar are the centers of these carpets. The majority of the surviving examples date from the 19th century and can be of either silk or wool pile (plate 5), however archaeological surveys have discovered considerably older carpet fragments in this region. These carpets synthesize the Turkic and Chinese symbols in colors that are much less subdued than those found in Chinese carpets (plate 235).

plate **5** | CHINESE
6'9" x 7' (2.06 x 2.13m)
A great example of simplicity of
Chinese rugs of the 19th century.

The Turkmen

Although much of the history of rug weaving can be traced through referring to the products of court looms and of the highest standards which have survived in museum and private collections, nomadic and village weavers have continued their weaving traditions throughout the centuries.

In Turkmenistan in Central Asia, weavers have continued to use their tribal ornaments of geometric rosettes, known as guls, arranged in symmetrical repeat patterns. These tribal emblems have totemic significance and seem to have changed little over the years. The tribes lead a nomadic existence in the desert areas of Central Asia and they made, as is the case with many village and tribal weavers, items that could be used in the course of daily life to cover floors or doors and act as containers for clothes, food etc. Woven items played an important part in the life of the community, especially the traditions attached to wedding ceremony and the bride's dowry.

The Turkmen are of diverse ethnic background but they continue a tradition of weaving in Central Asia that goes back to their ancestors the Ohguz Turks who later formed the Seljuk Empire. The different tribal guls used on their various woven products bear similarities to the roundels used on Seljuk, Chinese and Sasian art.

As no written records exist, what is known about these tribes has to be deduced from the records of 19th century Western travelers such as Aminius Vambery.

The Caucasus

In the seventh century B.C., the travelling historian Herodotus noted the ethnic diversity of the peoples of the Caucasus, and their skill in dyeing and weaving wool. Invaders had penetrated into the Caucasus through this North-South corridor from Derbent to Baku since the second millennium B.C., contributing with each successive wave to the wealth of ethnic groups who settled in this mountainous range.

More than three hundred distinct ethnic groups have survived in the remote regions of the Caucasus, a long-time refuge of peoples pushed out of more fertile or accessible lands. Many of these groups maintained their traditional identities and expressed them in their highly characteristic rug styles. Among the most important of these are the Circassians, Chechens, Lesghis, Persians, Kurds, and Armenians. The Armenian, settling in this area as far back as the sixth century B.C., were one of the earliest groups praised for their rug making, a tradition which persisted through the invasions of Khazars, Huns, and Avars. By the 13th century, the Seljuk Turks dominated most of Asia Minor and the Caucasus and in the seventeenth century the Safavids took control of the Southern regions. Thus it can be seen that the Caucasus is a melting pot of people and styles and influences.

The oldest surviving group of Caucasian rugs, the Dragon carpets, date from the 16th/17th centuries. These pieces have large lozenge-shaped compartments created by the intersections of lancet-like leaves. Within the compartments can be seen geometrized zoomorphs likened to dragons as well as phoenixes and other small animal figures depicted in brilliant blues, reds, and gold. The style is Persian in inspiration and influenced by the Safavid court carpets which have hunting scenes and animal combatants.

The successful Persian conquest of the Caucasus led to the division of the Caucasus in the 17th century into fifteen semi-independent Khanates (districts ruled by Khans), such as Gendje, Kuba, Karabagh, and other important rug-weaving districts. The influence of Russia in the region grew from the mid 19th century onwards and an expansion of the traditional handicrafts occurred. An example illustrating the mixture of the Persian and Russian influences can be seen in the 19th century Karabagh rug which has delightful rows of flowers on a navy field (plate 180).

Weaving in Europe

In the Europe, the large and varied output of knotted rugs and tapestries seems to originate from Near Eastern trade and diplomatic relations. Over the centuries, the indigenous European weaving traditions was established through the trade and contact with the great dyeing and weaving centers of the East through trading route: from North Africa to the Iberian peninsula; from Asia Minor through Middle and Eastern Europe and up to Scandinavia, and through the Mediterranean trading cities such as Venice.

The earliest known rug weaving center in Europe is in Lower Saxony which produced the Quedlinberg Carpet during the 12th century. Also Chinchilla in Spain is associated with the production of carpets dating to at least the 15th century. Since the Moorish conquest of Spain in the 12th century, Islamic culture ensured the spread of the decorative arts form throughout the peninsula.

From the 15th century the trading power of the Venetian merchants resulted in the regular appearance of rugs as luxury objects in European interiors and paintings. The paintings of Hans Holbein vividly testify to the popularity of Turkish rugs, which proliferated in churches, palaces, and wealthy homes. Turkish techniques were introduced into France and England and in England a domestic interpretation of pile called 'Turkey work' is well documented.

Carpet looms were established in France in the Louvre workshops in the 16th century and by the late 17th century, the workshops were moved to La Savonnerie at Chaillot, an old soap factory. The carpets made here and at Axminster marked the rise of a European style rug that would fit the architectural themes in vogue at the time and which are seen in the European palaces from the 17th century onwards.

plate **6**
'Ulysses finding Achilles
among the maidens'
English tapestry
18th century
7'4" x 17'4" (2.24 x 5.28m)

This, the sixth episode of seven in the mythological legend, the 'Story of Ulysses,' illustrates Ulysses (in Greek, Odysseus) finding Achilles among the maidens at the Court of Lycomedes. On the left in the open colonnade, Ulysses in disguise with Diomed offers musical instruments to the daughters of King Lycomedes. Four maidens are grouped around the seated Achilles, dressed in women's clothes. As he draws a sword from its sheath, two other maidens enter from the right.

The mythological sequence for this dynamic composition is compelling. When Achilles was a boy, a prophet predicted that he alone would conquer Troy. Achilles' mother, Thetis, soon realized that such a destiny would bring death upon her son. To protect him from the evident peril she hid him in the court of King Lycomedes, disguised as one of the maidens. Eventually the Greeks, helped by Ulysses, revealed Achilles' identity through an ingenious trick. Ulysses placed arms and armor amidst a display of women's finery and musical instruments that he presented to the daughters of Lycomedes. One story tells that Ulysses seized upon Achilles when he was the only 'maiden' to be fascinated by the swords and shields, whereas another version narrates that when Ulysses and his companions created battle cries and sounded the trumpets, Achilles, thinking they were being attacked, rushed for weapons. He then went willingly with the Greeks to attack Troy, for he could not escape his destiny.

This tapestry as identical to the example illustrated in Henry Currie Marillier, *English Tapestries of the 18th Century*, London: Medici Society, 1930, plate 42b. At the time of publication, known examples from the 'Story of Ulysses' series were limited to: one set of five pieces located at Hinwick House, Wellingborough, England; one set of three pieces formerly at the Spanish Art Gallery, one piece the former property of a Mr. Herrmann. A single fine copy of this tapestry with a different border and dimensions was located at Tylney Court, Hampshire.

Alongside the rug weaving tradition was an embroidery tradition that was well established in Europe when the Bayeaux tapestry was sewn in the 11th century. At Halberstadt in Germany there exists the fragments of 12th century tapestries woven locally and Upper Rhine tapestries are known to date from the 14th century. All these tapestries contributed to the growth of the tapestry weaving tradition of Europe which by the beginning of 15th century had become an important part of the furnishing of palaces.

The great European looms in places such as Tournai, Brussels, Aubusson and Gobelin in France and Flanders became more popular as they established a new style encouraged by the Renaissance and great patrons such as the Holy Roman Emperor, Charles V, and Henry II of France.

Scholarship

Oriental rugs first received scholarly attention in Europe but not until the 19th century. Wilhelm Von Bode, Ernest Kuhnel, Alois Riegl, and Arthur Upham Pope leading the way. Many early scholars poured their zeal as collectors into important studies, most notably the work of Arthur Urbane Dilley, Joseph V. McMullan, Maurice S. Dimand, Kurt Erdmann, and Cecil Edwards. This scholarship was the impetus behind major exhibitions, from the first important Oriental rug exhibition in Vienna in 1891 to the more recent exhibitions at the Textile Museum in Washington D.C. Although many rare rugs are in the hands of private collectors, most major museums have at least a few important pieces on exhibition.

Even though there is a large body of scholarship, dating rugs is still not an easy task. Rug weaving is a broad and complex field, singularly poor in documentation. A few records exist of conditions in the royal looms of Persia and Turkey, but many rugs were made by illiterate weavers who often copied dates as part of the design. So, although Islamic rugs occasionally bear dates, these should not be taken as necessarily accurate. Additionally any date conversion system must be used with considerable caution as in the 1920s, many Islamic countries adopted the Western calendar and in the 19th century occasionally the solar calendar.

The traditional Arabic system of dating started in 622 A.D., beginning with the flight of Mohammed from Mecca. It is based on the lunar year, which is longer than the Western solar year: the lunar year gains one solar year every 33.7 solar years. To convert an Islamic date, divide the inscribed date by 33.7; then add 622 to the inscribed date and from that result subtract the answer to the initial division date; this will be give you the Christian calendar date. A much simpler, although not as accurate conversion method is to add 583 to the Arabic date. It should be noted that Arabic dates appear in Arabic numerals and that these usually read from left to right.

The continuous tradition of copying older patterns further complicates the issues of attribution of Oriental rugs. However there are certain characteristics which when allied with the experience of seeing and touching thousands of rugs can be used to attribute most pieces with a certain amount of assurance: knowledge of dyes and structures and materials used in different weaving areas is key.

Despite this knowledge, scholars and dealers alike constantly disagree on nomenclature. Trade names are often misleading as an indication of the place where the rug was made, since they may only reflect the collection point or market place where the items were sourced or in cases such as the Princess Bukhara rugs, be just be apocryphal, as these rugs are made neither for royalty nor in the town of Bukhara.

plate 7
SILK AND METAL THREAD RUG
Istanbul District
19th century
4'3" x 6' (1.30 x 1.83m)
The use of silk and metal thread in weavings from Anatolia is usually associated with court production. The workshops around of Istanbul, Hereke, Kum Kapi all produced fine rugs that used silk and metal thread. There is a debate currently raging between scholars as to the origins and dating of a group of silk and metal thread rugs in the Tokapi palace: it is unsure whether they are 16th century Persian or 19th century Istanbul products. Despite this uncertainty it is clear that this rug is from the workshops creating commissions for the court at the early stages of the 19th century and follows in designs the ottoman court rugs of the 16th century.

History

The Materials and Techniques used in Rug Making

Materials

Many factors determine the quality of a carpet but the materials used to make it are those which are most easily controlled. These materials vary between regions however sheep's wool is most common and ubiquitous, as it is used for both pile and foundation.

In some regions camel, goat, horse and cow hair are used. These fibers form the pile along with wool or used as the only pile fiber. It is common to find these fibers used in the foundation of weavings made by rural or tribal communities: carpets from Hamadan region, usually known as Sarabs, use camel hair in the field for its durability; goat hair, appears as the warp threads of Turkmen weavings and as the side finishes of Baluch weavings. The soft, lustrous wool from the Angora goat, which is used in Turkish carpets, and pashmina, the extremely soft under fleece of the wild mountain goat used in very fine Persian rugs and a group of Indian Mughul carpets, are the most notable non-tribal uses of animal hair.

The quality of any wool can be affected by the breed, age, diet of the animal, the season of shearing, the part of the fleece sheared and the way that the sheared fleece is processed as well as the climate, altitude and type of the grazing: mountain sheep have longer fleeces; spring shearing yields a softer and finer wool, a winter one that is thicker and heavier; lamb's wool sheared between the eighth and fourteenth month is particularly fine, called *kork* in Persia; skin wool, sheared from a dead animal, is dry and loses its sheen and is used in low quality weaving.

When shearing it is important to maintain the maximum length of the wool fibers to allow for better dye saturation. Once completed, the wool is washed, sorted for length and coarseness and then teased and combed to separate and fluff the fibers. This unmats the wool so the fibers can then be combed out and spun into a thread form onto a drop spindle or spinning wheel. The handspinning of the thread creates a strong yarn with a texture that cannot be achieved by machine and creates a texture which is desirable in antique carpets and indeed distinguishes the hand-made carpet from machine made products. The yarn is ready to be dyed.

Cotton is used for the foundation of many rugs but is sometimes seen in the pile of rugs: in some Turkmen rugs it is used for white highlights. Cotton is stronger than wool and is not subject to the same shrinkage as wool and therefore irregular shapes are avoided when used in the foundation. In the late 19th century machine-spun cotton began to be used whereas before it had been hand-spun locally: some experts can tell the differences in appearance of these two types of cotton yarns and use this to date rugs. In some carpets, like some 19th century rugs from Turkey, 'polished' cotton appears in the pile which looks like silk, but in fact is mercerized cotton - cotton treated with alkali solutions.

Silk is used in more expensive pieces for either pile or foundation or sometimes both. It is much admired for its beauty and luster, and it allows an extremely fine weave. It was used in Turkish court prayer rugs and for both pile and foundation in a body of Northwest Persian carpets in the second half of the 19th century. Unfortunately, warm and/or humid conditions can bring about dry rot, which disintegrates the structure and knotting of silk rugs. The only other fibers sometimes used in carpets are hemp and jute both of which are used in the foundation.

Dyes

An expert can use dyes, both natural and synthetic, to date and attribute carpets. The majority of the pieces illustrated in this book contain natural dyes, however many rugs made from the late 19th century onwards contain synthetic dyes. These dyes were developed in Europe in the 19th century and first appeared in rugs-weaving areas in the late 1860s. However they were in more widespread use in the last twenty years of the 19th century. Until then all the dyes used had come from the natural world.

Many connoisseurs consider that the arrival of synthetic dyes mark the ending of authentic tribal weavings, since these dyes signal the influence of an alien culture and hence the dilution of nature tradition. Many dealers and collectors will not seriously consider a rug with synthetic colors, their introduction serves as a qualitative watershed: the depth of color of natural dyes is unmistakable. However it is now hard to spot the difference between the new generation of synthetic dyes and natural dyes.

Natural dyes have been used for millennia and along with spices have formed an important item of trade between disparate cultures. For example, the Phoenicians developed the famous and costly 'real' purple dye from shellfish which imparted prestige on those that wore them from Roman times up until the end of the Byzantine Empire. The international trade routes transported the dyestuffs across the world. Master-dyers were held in high esteem and the dye recipes remained the property of secret guilds: many medieval rulers in the Islamic world built dye-houses into their palace complexes. Although prestigious weavings contain the most desirable colors and expensive dyes, many antique carpets are dyed by materials available within the region and are inextricably linked to those traditions.

Many natural dyes need a mordant to work. This facilitates the attachment of the dye onto the material to be dyed. Some dyes do not need mordanting as the dye and wool need only to be put together in a vat. In the case of dyeing brown or black a ferrous mordant is used which weakens the wool and leads it to corrode, leaving what looks like wear. Since brown or black are often used to outline designs, if this corrosion occurs a sculpted or relief effect is given to the design element which is considered quite desirable and is used as a means of helping date carpets.

There are inconsistencies that occur during dyeing which become more pronounced when seen in a rug or carpet. Variations in color saturation called an Abrash occur through the differing length of times that the material is immersed or different weights of wool or temperature or measures of dye between dye-batches. Although it looks like a mistake it also has the beneficial effect of creating a unique colorway for each rug and a varying depth to the color which can add a three dimensionality to the design. The fastness of the natural dyes varies a great deal, but usually if well applied, the colors undergo a gentle mellowing over the years.

A considerable range of natural ingredients has been used for dyeing. The two most commons are madder for red and indigo for blue. The madder plant grows wild throughout the Near East and Central Asia, the dye is extracted from its roots. It provides a wide spectrum of reds from pale brick red to deep plum. The process of dyeing wool red takes one to two days of soaking the skeins of wool, which have been previously boiled in an alum mordant, in a solution of dried and ground madder root. The colors produced hold very fast to light and washing. Varying the amount of dye or adding additional substances can produce different shades: the addition of tin to the madder and alum mordant produces a distinctive pink.

Another source of red is from cochineal which produces a blue red. This is derived from the crushed bodies of a Central American insect introduced into Spain in the 17th century and thence into the rug-weaving areas in the 19th century. A very similar color is produced by the use of an insect found in Indian Lac tree which is often found in old Kerman and Khorassan rugs.

Blue is derived from the indigo plant, which is thought to have originated from India. A great number of hues can be obtained through variations in the complex fermentation process which involves indigo, clay, slaked lime, sugar, animal urine and potash. Indigo, unlike other dyes, darkens with age and acts as a preservative so that in many old rugs, if unworn, the level of the indigo-dyed wool has stayed constant over time. After 1880, a synthetic indigo came into use which is chemically identical and indistinguishable from natural indigo.

Other colors are produced by using other dyestuffs or by over-dyeing the shades already dyed. Saffron produces the brightest yellow, however its expense limits its use. A milder yellow is obtained from weld, extracted from a vine of the *reseda* family; sumac, turmeric, and pomegranate rind also provide various yellows; buck thorn is the yellow most favored by dyers of the Caucasus. Greens could be mixed from a bath of indigo followed by a bath of yellow dye. The henna plant, long used for dyeing human hair and skin, produces a rich orange seen in late 19th century Turkish and Moroccan rugs.

White, black, and brown come from natural wool color, but these colors can with difficulty be dyed. Brown is obtained from a walnut husk or a gallnut base. A bath in madder also achieves a reddish brown. Sometimes even natural colored wool requires special treatment, bleaching in the case of white wool, for example.

The first artificial dyes were synthesized in 1856. These were acid, coal-tar derivative dyes which made the wool stiffer and drier, and the colors tended to run and fade. The earliest colors produced were mauve and two magentas; the introduction of azo dyes followed in 1864, and alizarin reds came into use about the same time. A dyed called fucsine is the first seen in rugs which is purple which on the front of the rug fades to blue/gray.

The fugitive qualities of these early synthetics meant that within a few years the colors would disappear from rugs and if wetted they would run into other colors or stain. Therefore about ten years after their introduction late in the 19th century, severe laws restricting their use were enacted in Persia in order to maintain the quality of their exports. New generations of more stable synthetic dyes gradually became available and came to dominate rug dyeing. Chrome dyes produced a wide range of colors resistant to water and sunlight and age.

The differences in taste of the rug-buying nations, in terms of color and design, had a more direct effect on the rug-weaving nations from the late 19th century onwards. The harshness or brightness of synthetic colors was not desirable in some countries so to mellow the colors chemical washing created the lightness of color desired. This bleaching also allowed for colors to be changed through re-coloring the carpet with fabric paint. These practices were used in Mahal and Sarouk carpets exported to the United States in the 1920s and in Kerman rugs of the 1960s: the strong reds in these carpets were bleached to milder rose tones, which were occasionally painted by hand to a more somber maroon shade.

Techniques of Weaving

The basic formula for making rugs has certain variations, but essentially has not changed for centuries. Pile rugs are made according to the ancient method which combines weaving and knotting.

The wool or cotton threads are spun into yarns then a number of these yarns are spun together to form a thick thread. The direction in which these yarns are twisted or plied, either clockwise or anti-clockwise, is one method used to help experts attribute some weavings to certain areas.

The materials used for the warp are usually the thickest of the threads made. The warp runs along the length of the rug and the weft across the fabric, evenly from side to side; the weft is thinner than the warp, contains fewer constituent yarns which may not even be properly plied together.

The most basic weave is a balanced plainweave. This involves the wefts travelling from one side of the width of the weaving to the other by passing over one warp and then under the next, in an undulating motion thereby interlacing the warps. The finished product has a pattern formed through the equal exposure of the warp and weft - in other words balanced. Although this method is referred to as flatweaving, it is tapestry weaving in its simplest form.

The various types of tapestry weaving are distinguished by the method used to produce the pattern and changes of color. Most kilims or flatwoven products from the Middle East are called weft-faced weaves since the pattern is produced by the exposure of the weft and the addition of supplementary colored wefts. The techniques used to make a tapestry, in the sense of the European pictorial hanging, and a kilim from Iran are essentially the same. The varieties of weft-faced weaves are too complex to discuss here, however one technique commonly found in oriental weaving is that of sumakh: this involves passing an extra weft over four warps, then back under two, the unused threads are carried over on the back of the rug leaving an effect similar to that seen on the back of an embroidery. Unlike a kilim, the pattern on a sumakh as seen on the front of the weaving cannot be clearly seen on the back, since the mass of carried threads obscure the clear view of any distinct patterning, thus the sumakh can only be used on one side, unlike a kilim. These different methods of flatweaving are sometimes used on the ends of rugs when they are removed from the loom, these end finishes vary depending on the locality.

plate **8**
SHAHSAWAN PILLOW COVER

plate **9**
SADDLE BAG

Knots

fig **1** | Turkish knot

fig **2** | Persian knot

The pile or knots which characterize rugs are a form of extra-weft wrapping. The knotting thread is wrapped around two warps; exceptions to this are the *jufti* knot which is wrapped around four warps as a time-saving device but yields a weaker product more prone to wear, and the Spanish knot which is tied around a single warp. Each row of knots is separated by wefts which undulate between the warps and are beaten down with a comb to secure the preceding row of knots. The number of wefts used varies from one to eight or more. The number and color of the wefts used is another means of identification for rugs.

Several types of knots are used and although some are named after certain areas, some weaving centers use more than one type. The Turkish, or Ghiordes, knot is wrapped around two adjacent warps so that the ends emerge in the space between them, this knot has come to be called the symmetric knot (see fig. 1 Turkish knot). The Persian, or Senneh, knot wraps around one warp with the yarn passing behind the adjacent warp so that it collars the warps exactly as a single uncovered warp divides the two pile ends, this knot has come to be called the asymmetric knot (see fig. 2 Persian knot); if the uncovered warp is the left one of the two warps the knot is referred to asymmetric open to the left and asymmetric open to the right if the right warp is uncovered or open.

The Turkish knot grips the warp threads more firmly yet allows for less fine curvilinear designs. The Persian knot allows for more knots to be contained within a given area, and therefore is used for more curvilinear and detailed designs. Sometimes one warp is pulled much tighter than any of the others which displaces it from its adjacent position. This is a characteristic of rugs with the Persian knot and its effect can be seen though a pronounced ridged effect on the back of the rug. This displacement can make it difficult to see the main body of the knot as the warps can lie almost on top of each other.

The simplest loom consists of two beams staked to the ground, with the warp stretched between them. A device called a shed separates alternate warps, so that the weft may pass easily between them. The weaver usually squats in front of the loom, or may sit on a plank supported by two stones on either side of the work in progress. This type of loom limits the size of rugs to a width of four or five feet and is typically used by nomads because it is light and allows for the loom to be moved easily even with a rug still on the loom.

There are several types of upright looms, used in villages and town workshops, which allow the weaver to work at eye level to the rug and to make large carpets. One type has a fixed upper beam and a moveable lower cloth beam which fits into slots in the vertical side-pieces. Another, the Tabriz loom, features adjustable warps wound around the top of the frame, so that the rugs may be shifted and pulled down around the back of the loom.

The weaver requires only a few simple tools: an iron comb packs down each row of wefts; a knife with a small hook at one end to loop the pile yarn around the warps and is then cut to make the pile; a pair of shears trims the pile. The average rate of production depends on the fineness of the rug and the weavers' skill but a rough guideline is that 1,400 knots per day will produce about one square meter in four months.

Traditionally, the art of weaving has been passed on from mother to daughter, but in larger workshops, the weaving proceeds under the guidance of a master (Mo'allem) who knows many patterns and chants them to the weavers or the patterns have been transcribed into a paper called a cartoon.

Design

Although rug weaving is thousands of years old and has become an important tradition to many different cultures, several basic formats have remained dominant, the most common being that of a field contained by borders. The origins of this format are uncertain but since the ends and sides need to be treated differently to the rest of the weaving so that the piece is secure, perhaps the medium itself has dictated this format. Equally the borders frames the field in a manner similar to that found in paintings and could have been adopted as a standard artistic tool to emphasize and delineate a decorated space.

This format is particularly suitable for use of square or rectangular shape. However many weavings which differ from the typical rectangular shape still use the border and field relationship: for example the five sided Turkmen *asmalyk*, which are made in pairs and decorate the flanks of the camel during the bridal procession, retain the field and borders format.

A major border is flanked by minor ones and then guards' stripes. Each of these has less elaboration corresponding to their size. The major, and sometimes the minor borders, contains a repeat of floral or geometric elements or a meandering vine design. A rug's origin may be deduced by looking at the borders as some areas use only a few variants. The corners of the borders also reveal whether the rug was woven from memory or from a cartoon or copied from another rug because it is difficult to take a design around the corner without interrupting the flow; a designer will have solved this problem at the outset. The improvisation seen in some tribal rugs is a quality that many collectors admire.

The field of a rug may feature an all-over free flowing design, a symmetric repeat of floral clusters, a lattice or grid or frequently a medallion dominating the center which may, as is seen in Caucasian rugs, be repeated. A single medallion is usually repeated in quarters in the corner of the field and the medallion may have pendants attached above and below it. Many all-over designs are cut-off by the borders, suggesting that the field is a selected views of a pattern that is an infinitely repeating, an idea important to and often found in Islamic art. In pictorial rugs, the central field contains hunting scenes, animals, the tree of life, vase or fountain motifs, as well as historic narratives and occasionally in the 20th century, commemorative portraits. However within all these milieu, symmetry plays a major role in the organization of a rug design.

One of the easiest oriental carpet designs to recognize is the prayer rug which has an asymmetric design. The field has an arch or *mihrab* at its top inspired by the architecture of the mosque; the prayer arch which directs the worshipper to face towards Mecca. This design is directional and gives the rug an obvious orientation. In some rugs these arches have become purely a decorative element but in others there are elements which are related to the points at which hands, knees and feet and head touch the rug or ground during supplication.

The treatment of design elements is either curvilinear or rectilinear: curvilinear designs tend to represent natural forms; rectilinear designs are more abstract in their representation. Originally patterns were particular to certain regions, however the growth in large scale carpet production, during the second half of the 19th century, known as 'the revival period' in Persia, meant that many designs were used outside their places of origin, and were frequently adapted to Western taste. Consequently, design alone is not an adequate criterion for judging a carpet's place of manufacture.

Use and Application

Although wall-to-wall carpeting and machine-made rugs dominated the market in the 1950s and 1960s, the 2000s have signaled a return to favor for the handmade rug. Unlike wall-to-wall carpeting, which is short-lived and difficult to uproot, rugs are long lasting and flexible since they can be moved and reused in new contexts. In addition, handmade carpets can be sold when the owner needs to move, or becomes tired of the piece.

Modern architects and interior designers use rugs as one of the primary tools to organize space. Rugs and tapestries add focus and context to groups of furniture, articulate space, and enhance architecture. Rugs serve as a means of dividing a room without creating physical barriers; in a large unmodified area, a loft or a large living room, small rugs break up the space to define living or working spaces; the color and design of rugs can unify antique and contemporary furniture creating a provocative juxtaposition; leaving space between the edge of a rug and the wall on the floor produces an sense of space and light; rich colors draw attention away from low ceilings giving the appearance of height to a room.

Interior designers recognize that rugs and carpets can create a variety of moods, as well as meet practical needs: thick pile rugs, with brilliant colors and bold designs, such as Kazaks, Shirvans and other Caucasian rugs, create a feeling of warmth; Ushak and Agra carpets work equally well in formal and informal environments; the light pastel colors in Ushaks and Sultanabad carpets suggest a cool, summery, open and relaxed effect and are much favored in warm climates and summer homes; Heriz, Serapis, and many nineteenth-century Chinese rugs offer flexibility in mixing modern and antique furniture without creating a conflict.

As traditional floor coverings, handmade rugs introduce a note of originality and distinction into the home or office. Innovative designers have used rugs as hangings over balconies, as table tops pressed under glass or Lucite, as cushion and sofa covers. Several corporate art curators and architects, given the comparatively lower cost of rugs as art in relation to second string paintings, have elected to hang fine rugs or tapestries in boardrooms and executive offices.

Care & Restoration

Many people believe that cleaning may damage a rug, but rugs are extremely robust. In many parts of the Middle East, rugs were washed in local streams with heavy soap and left to dry in the sun, or, in winter, were turned face down on the snow and vigorously beaten. Cleaning has become much more sophisticated and can actually prolong the life of a rug. However many commercial rug shampoos dehydrate the pile and fail to clean deeply. Anyway it is difficult to dry rugs adequately at home, and damp may promote decay. To this end it is important that the best professional advice and services are sought. The specialized cleaning of valuable antiques is almost an art in itself.

Several steps can be taken at home to aid the rug's longevity. A foam rubber pad should be placed under the rug to prevent slippage, and to safeguard against wear caused by the friction of the rug against a hard surface. Such pads are available from most dealers at a low cost. Also try to place a rug in a low traffic area and if any wear is likely to occur then move the rug around to ensure even rather than concentrated wear.

If a rug or tapestry is hung, avoid hooks and nails which may damage the foundations or result in scalloping. A pole strung through a backing or Velcro tape will allow for a more even distribution of weight. All rugs, including those you might have hanging, collect dust and should be vacuumed with the air draft hose. Vacuuming on both sides removes more of the dirt. Any animal spot or stain should be taken care of immediately with plain cold water applied in the soiled area to avoid spreading harmful substances. In addition the lighting of the hung piece should be considered just as one would if it were a painting.

Persian Rugs

'The very word *Persian* is a synonym for opulence, splendour, gorgeousness; and *Oriental* means beauty and wonder and the magic of the *Arabian Nights*. From the Alladin's cave of the mystical East, therefore, we may still hope to gather treasure and spoil.' (*The Oriental Rug* by W.D.Ellwanger. Dodd, Mead & Company, 1903)

Persia occupies a pivotal position among the rugproducing countries, with Turkey to the West, the Caucasus to the North, and Afghanistan and central Asia to the East. In the 17th century, the Safavid Empire stretched beyond present-day Iran to include parts of Western Afghanistan, Azerbaijan, Iraq and Syria, and its cultural influence was felt throughout the region. This land rises to form a vast plateau reaching an elevation of roughly four thousand feet in Western Asia.

The term Persian has become synonymous with oriental rugs, since in the 19th and early 20th centuries Persia became the largest exporter of rugs to the West. The distinct designs of Persian carpets and the envied quality of Persian wool and dyes coupled with a tradition of fine craftsmanship have earned these rugs their reputation as the finest examples of the knotted art. Although the intricacy of many Persian rugs woven in city workshops, have established a standard of quality for Persian rugs that is recognized throughout the world, it is not so much the fineness of weave that indicates a rug's quality in antique examples, but more, an appreciation of the combined factors of its material, aesthetic quality, and relative rarity within its weaving type or group.

The history of the Persian people is very much reflected in the weavings that it produces. For example, there are in the South of Persia Arabs that are descendants of the early Arab invaders, and large parts of the rural population are of Turkic racial origin, and still speak Turkic languages. The carpets that they produce incorporate individual elements that are typical of their ancestral weavings.

The Senneh and Ghiordes knots are used throughout Persia, sometimes in the same region. The traditions of the city workshops are derived from a court tradition established to serve the demands during the Safavid period. The rural and tribal traditions share this common cultural heritage with their own older and less formalized tradition.

Despite the wealth of diversity found in Persian rug weaving, Persian rugs are highly distinctive with the formality of their elegant designs; they favor curvilinear floral motifs and crisp, symmetrically arranged medallions. The intricate detail expressed by flowing curves is at once distinguishable from the more geometric devices used on the neighboring rugs of Turkey and the Caucasus.

The golden age of Persian carpet weaving was during the Safavid era in the 16th and 17th centuries. Until mid-19th century there was little weaving industry to speak of apart from small-scale local product. In the latter half of the 19th century, a surge in Western demand for oriental rugs brought a fresh interest in older Persian carpets. The astute dealers of Tabriz started buying up old Persian carpets and shipping them to Istanbul for the Western market in the 1860s. When they realized that they were running out of old carpets to buy, they industriously decided to make their own. The looms began to emerge in the old centers of the textile trade in places like Kerman, Khorassan, Sultanabad, Kashan. The areas around the Azerbaijani capital Tabriz produced many carpets collected in towns like Heriz, Karadja, Meskin, and Bakhshayesh.

By the 1880s, foreign firms opened their own factories, such as Petag in Tabriz and Ziegler in Sultanabad. They strictly controlled colors and designs by providing ready-dyed wool and supplying weavers with cartoons. They also made carpet better suited for the Western market by dictating larger size carpets than were usually woven for local consumption. These designs gained popularity in the West and inspired many similar carpets made in the areas in which the European weaving companies were based. Though in many cases no signature exists in the rug, the influence of some of the individual masterweavers of this Revival period such as the Mohtashem Kashan, the Dabir Kashan, and the Hajji Jalili Tabriz are recognizable to most experts. Occasionally, European and American buyers had their company names knotted into rugs: the best known of these are Costigian, Ghastili, Dilmaghani of Kerman, Taftanchian in Kerman and Arak and Amoghli and Saber in Mashad.

The development and subsequent regional attribution of a Persian rug design is very difficult, since designs were copied according to fashion and popularity at this time. The weaving of many large carpets and rugs was an export-led industry. However this existed alongside a regional tradition. In the following brief survey, we shall only deal with the major prolific rug-producing centers by geographic area.

Northwest Persia

A great variety of rugs have been produced over the last hundred years in the Northwest of Persia in the areas historically known as Persian Kurdistan, Azerbaijan and Armenia. This area incorporates some of the most prolific carpet weaving centers in Persia during the second half of the 19th century.

Tabriz in the Northwest of Persia was the capital of the ancient Mongol Empire and the first capital of the Safavid Empire and has flourished as a rug center since the 15th and 16th centuries. Today it is the capital of Persian Azerbaijan and Iran's second largest city. During its long history the Sultans of Turkey and the Shahs of Persia have requisitioned its weavers. A group of important medallion carpets were made there in the 16th century which are the starting point of the Safavid carpet weaving tradition. Recent research suggests that Tabriz may be responsible for a greater part in the weaving of classical carpets that was first thought, including the so-called dragon carpets.

The weavers of Tabriz did not produced as many carpets in the Revival period as those of Hamadan and Arak, but the ones that it did produce are recognized for their quality. Tabriz merchants were, as has been mentioned, responsible for establishing manufacture of carpets in the 1860s, therefore it is not surprising that many of the looms in Tabriz were established in large workshops rather than weavers homes. Tabriz merchants were thus able to control their production very closely and also produce many large room-sized carpets. Tabriz weavers have long had a reputation for copying designs from other areas, such as those of Sultanabad and Anatolia. The growth of the weaving for export industry meant that Tabriz could produce a greater variety of weavings and patterns than other areas. Often a structural examination is necessary to establish that a carpet has been made in Tabriz. These carpets, from the second half of 19th century at least, have an all cotton foundation with two wefts and a symmetric knot.

The German firm Petag established looms and production in Tabriz following the success of the local merchants. These and certain other Tabriz carpets can be recognized through their quality and design. The work of one masterweaver, Hajji Jalili, from the town of Marand, has received particular recognition as the most famous weaver working in Tabriz around the turn of the 20th century (plates 52, 53). He produced very fine versions of historical designs, such as the Ardebil (plate 50). Characteristic of Jalili's style is very finely knotted medallion designs done in soft colors, occasionally in silk, with short pile and precise drawing. Lately this name has come to use as term of quality and is ascribed less specifically to a certain quality of Tabriz carpet rather than to the specific works of Hajji Jalili himself (plates 10, 51).

In the last decades of the 19th century and through to today, Tabriz weavers produced silk rugs and carpets, some of massive proportions, which are highly valued today. These rugs are made entirely from silk and have symmetric knots. Medallion designs are common, as are interpretations of Anatolia prayer rugs complete with hanging lamps and columns.

Just northeast of Tabriz lies a group of about thirty villages, the largest and most important of which is Heriz. Heriz was the collecting point for the products of the surrounding villages and consequently gave its name to the region's weavings. These villages were, and still are, responsible for producing a great volume of carpets which were exported to the West in the late 19th and early 20th centuries. The looms were established again by the enterprising Tabriz merchants (plates 11, 12, 67).

The weavers of Heriz also produced sumptuous silk rugs during the second half of the 19th and early in the 20th century. The output of silk carpets was limited, resulting in high prices for the surviving examples. They are similar in weave to Tabriz silk rugs but are usually more curvilinear in design and have a madder red coloring.

Wool rugs produced with the same care can equally convey such elegance and are much sought after. Typically, Heriz rugs have a medallion design and have a preponderance of madder red, indigo blue along with white and yellow details. Early 19th century rugs are rare and have a wool rather than cotton foundation. The United States imported many late 19th century Heriz rugs at the turn of the 20th century. These rugs impress us with their crisply designed medallions and the stylized elements in the design that seem to be of a zoomorphic nature.

Some of the weavings of the surrounding area can be identified without too much difficulty. The name Serapi is used in relation to the best Heriz carpets which are more finely knotted and have more boldly con-

plate **10** | TABRIZ RUG
Northwest Persia
19th century
4'5" x 5'7" (1.35 x 1.70m)
This prayer rug has an elaborate mihrab form and stylized flowering vase. This design, with the accompanying flute-playing monkey-like figures, is more usually found in silk.

ceived medallion designs in crystalline colors (plates 55, 58, 59, 60, 61, 62, 69, 71). Serapis sometimes have cartouches in their borders containing poems and other inscriptions (plate 59); dignitaries usually commissioned such pieces for special occasions. Although recently the term Serapi is attached to any old Heriz carpet, the term does apply technically to an older generation of carpets which have depressed warps. The coarser, less costly grades from the Heriz area go by the name of Gorevan. The design of these rugs is similar to the better grades, but the weave is less fine and colors and wool are harsher.

The village of Bakhshaish, located between Tabriz and Heriz, produces mainly large rugs and carpets. Their villagey, less formalized designs, soft colors and bold one-way designs are avidly sought, and a Kurdish influence can be seen in the 19th century production (plates 56, 68, 70). A wool foundation was used and the Herati design is common, these rugs maintain a less commercial design reportoire and therefore have a charm admired by many. The output of these lustrous and perennially popular rugs was limited and came to an end in the early 20th century.

In the extreme East of Azerbaijan is Ardebil, famous for the two renowned 16th century pieces, now held by the Victoria & Albert Museum in London, and the Los Angeles County Museum of Art in Los Angeles. The rugs were found in a royal shrine outside the town, but it is generally agreed that these carpets were not made in Ardebil, although there were

plate **11** | HERIZ CARPET
Northwest Persia
Late 19th century
8' x 10'7" (2.44 x 3.23m)
This all-over herati design is unusual in Heriz carpets, as is the particularly light coloration of the field. The breadth of the field design is matched perfectly by the space seen in the meandering vine and samovar border. A carpet of subtle design and palette of the sort that is much in demand.

carpets produced there in the 20th century (plate 13). These borrow heavily from the geometrical Caucasian design and are produced in large numbers. In the North of the region, located on the Persian side of the Caucasian border, the town of Meshkin has been the source of mass-produced copies of Caucasian carpets along with hardwearing runners.

Outside the immediate Heriz weaving district is the town of Karadja, between Heriz and Tabriz. Karadja produced a larger amount of small rugs and runners than its neighboring Heriz. Larger Karadja rugs are unusual and as all Karadja weavings, are single wafted. The identification of the particular medallion types of the weavings from this town and a few surrounding villages are usually enough to allow for clear identification (plates 64, 65).

The village of Serab specialized in producing runners. Serab runners have often been mistakenly referred to as having camel wool in them because of the camel/beige ground color which is produced by dyeing the wool with walnut husks. Rugs from this area are rare and since Western tastes of the 19th and 20th century favored bolder colors, only a handful

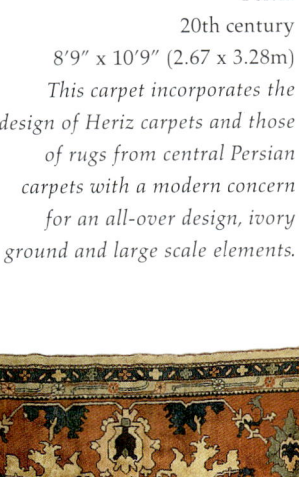

plate **12** | Heriz design carpet
Persia
20th century
8′9″ x 10′9″ (2.67 x 3.28m)
This carpet incorporates the design of Heriz carpets and those of rugs from central Persian carpets with a modern concern for an all-over design, ivory ground and large scale elements.

plate **13** | Ardebil Carpet
Northwest Persia
20th century
5′2″ x 9′1″ (1.57 x 2.77m)
This is not typical of the weavings of Ardebil but the tone on tone color gives the geometric pattern an attractive subtlety.

of these well-made runners have reached the Western market. Naturally, these examples are highly prized by collectors (plate 66).

The name Shahsavan, is the name given to a confederation of tribes assembled by Shah Abbas in the 17th century in order to dilute the power of the individual tribes, and to act as a buffer against incursions by aggressors in the Northwest. The name literally means, 'those that love the Shah.' These nomadic tribesmen made fine flat-weave carpets, bags, and other items for domestic use, however there was also a settled minority that made pile rugs which are usually referred to as Northwest Persian rather than anything more specific. Shahsavan weavings are often colorful and have a design vocabulary that shares much in common with Caucasian rugs.

West and Central Persian

This area is Persian Kurdistan. Rugs woven by Kurds can be very diverse, ranging from woolly and coarse, true village products, to some of the finest woven rugs of Persia. They are difficult to identify in terms of tribal groups, but some are attributed to specific centers of manufacture, such as Mosul or Sauj Bulak (plate 74). Today, semi-nomadic Kurds produce a number of different rug types, and their utility bags are increasingly prized by collectors. Kurdistan has a reputation for using lustrous wool and traditional vegetable dyes. For centuries the Kurds not only of Persia, but also Turkey, Iraq, Syria, Armenia, and Azerbaijan have opposed their rulers. From the Safavid era until the 18th century, important carpet makers of Kurdish origin were deported en masse to remote border areas of Persia, such as Khorassan, where the borders of Russia, Afghanistan and Iran meet.

Some of the best Kurdish rugs come from Bijar (plates 29, 34, 39, 41, 42, 76). These rugs are extremely tightly woven and tolerant to the hardest use. They are sturdy and longwearing, and often referred to as the 'Iron rugs of Persia,' since the multiple filler wefts that are inserted between rows of knots are very tightly packed and beaten down by a special comb. The result is a rug of lustrous and velvety texture which is inflexible and tight. The Bijars are also known for their rich, deep colors, a characteristic of many Kurdish rugs. The weavers favor large room and corridor sizes in medallion designs and floral repeats, as well as the Western floral pattern called 'Gul Farangs' ('European roses') (plates 31, 39). This pattern is by no means exclusive to the Bidjar area, also often found in the rugs of Afshar, Karabagh, Kerman, Senneh and Kazak. This illustrates the reason we should not ascribe rug origins by design alone. An interesting and rare Bidjar Sampler or Vagireh is featured in plate 28.

One type of Bijar rug has a field design of split arabesques and is believed to be made in the small town of Garrus. Their design vocabulary indicates that this area is still weaving patterns that are directly inherited from Safavid traditions, as these all-over arabesque forms are seen in a specific group of Safavid rugs.

Some of the most famous Persian carpets, due to their extremely fine weave and mesmerizing intricacy of design, are Sennehs, made in a city now called Sanandag. Since Nadir Shah declared Senneh the capital of Kurdistan in the 18th century, its products have been much desired. The rugs are thinner and more pliable than other Persian rugs because of their often very fine knotting (up to 400 per square inch), thin warp of cotton or silk, and single weft. Ironically, although Senneh gave its name to the knot also known as Persian or asymmetrical, many of the rugs woven in the area use the Turkish knot. The importance of Senneh carpets relates to their refinement of weaving, pattern and coloring. Smaller sizes of these rugs with minute floral patterns are favored, in combination with medallion designs. The delicate color palette rests on sandy tones, pinks, ivory, and indigo. Many earlier Senneh rugs are woven with 'Haft Rang', or rainbow warps, using rows of seven colors of silk threads. Many rugs were woven for royal courts, sometimes referred to as Fatalishah or Audience carpets (plate 36). The Khan, a person of great importance, would be seated at the head of the rug, the central walkway was for visitors and town people to came to pay respect to the Khan, while servants and bodyguards flanked both sides of this walkway. This is a representation of a set of two main rugs, flanked by a pair of runners. These sets of rugs, here woven together, are an illustration of the use of and shapes of carpets found traditionally in Persia.

Senneh is also famous for the weaving some of the finest of kilims made anywhere which are occasionally but very rarely all silk (plates 30, 37). These kilims, due to their beauty and rarity are the some of the most sought after and collected weavings from the Persian repertoire. Also, as a consequence of their fragile nature, old examples are rare and expensive. Finally, the villages surrounding the urban weaving centers of Senneh also produce many rugs which are identified in the trade as Kurdish.

To the Southwest of Senneh is the province and city of Hamadan which sits in the center of a large rug-producing area of hundreds of villages and thousands of looms. In ancient time, Hamadan was a city of considerable importance, and the region has long been one of the largest producers of carpets; A. Cecil Edwards estimated that there must have been over 30,000 looms in the region of Hamadan after the First World War. Coarse rugs of small or scatter sizes were and are made in this region in the many villages which incorporate Kurdish and Persian populations. There are different types of rugs that can be identified as being from particular sources, such as Borchalu, Tafrish or Ingeles but all have in common a single weft, an all cotton foundation, and symmetric knots. Longer-pile rugs, often with geometric patterns and somber colors, including runners framed by a characteristic plain camel colored border are some of the more common types seen in the marketplace. The collecting point of these rugs was the city of Hamadan, therefore Hamadan has become a generic term for rugs from this area.

plate **15** | Ziegler Mahal Carpet
West Persia
Late 19th century
6' x 8' (1.83 x 2.44m)
*Small Zieglers are unusual and
this captures all that is great in
the larger carpets in terms of
color, quality of design rendition
and the balance of colors between
the field and borders.*

plate **14** | Bijar Runner
West Persia
19th century
4'6" x 12' (1.37 x 3.66m)
*A beautiful village weaving in
the saturated colors of the
Kurdish weaving repertoire. The
Mina khani design is a favorite
of this weaving region and a
sense of vitality is imparted into
the design by the looseness of the
drawing. The border is one that is
associated with an older type of
Bijar weaving.*

Situated in the South of the Hamadan region, the town of Malayer produces good quality rugs using the Turkish knot. Malayer rugs made before 1935 enjoy much prestige among carpet connoisseurs and are regarded as far more praiseworthy than other Hamadan rugs (plate 33, 47, 49, 82). The most important of Malayer rugs are the Mishan Malayers, which are superb in subtlety of color and design and fineness of the weave. Consequently, these carpets command much higher regard then the average Malayers (plates 45, 46).

Southeast of the Hamadan is the region of Arak, another of Persia 's prolific weaving areas. The people of Arak are more Persian in their culture and origin that the Turkic and mixed ethnic make-up of the Northwest.

The older carpets from this area are called Farahan after the plain of that name. These carpets were made in classic designs such as the Herati, Mustophi and Mina Khani (plates 44, 81, 83) with deep colors including a deep indigo ground color and a bright but corrosive green, commonly called pistachio green. Many of these were large carpets made in workshops rather than homes, with medallion designs rare. Farahan carpets were some of the first carpets to arrive in the West in the second half of the 19th century, their large sizes leading themselves to use in stately homes throughout Europe. When the boom in exporting came in 1870s, these workshops were taken over and enlarged by Western firms, the most famous of these being Ziegler & Company.

This Manchester based firm became involved in carpet production in Sultanabad, in the province of Arak, in 1882. The degree of their influence can be seen by their involvement in getting the famous Ardebil carpet out of Iran. Their company produced some of the most important carpets made in the late 19th century for the export market. The company created its own design cartoons and gave their weavers ready-dyed wool and exact patterns to weave. In this way and through the security of their compound the company managed to weave designs and colorways that were exactly suited to Western interiors (plates 15, 16). An often-seen design from this manufacturer is a red field adorned with the 'Gul Hana' (Henna) flower repeat, surrounded by a dark blue border with soft greens, and yellow highlights (plate 89). Great effort has been made to reproduce those designs, sometimes with lighter colors than the original, in different parts of the world: in Iran, Turkey, Egypt, and even Romania.

Generally, the rugs from the Arak, formerly called Sultanabad (plate 93), region are not as tightly woven as other Persian rugs, but they quite often feature some of the most beautiful and creative color combinations found in Persian rugs, so much so that these are the first choice of many dealers and decorators. Mahal rugs are made in the same area and are often called Sultanabad to command higher prices, but in fact, Mahal denotes a grade of weave which is flatter, the warps lie side by side in the woven structure, and are looser than other weavings of the district (plates 17, 25, 35, 84, 86, 87, 91). In Iran today, Mushkabad is the proper name for rugs of this area, the old Mahal rugs being lighter in weight and looser in their weave than these modern counterparts. The old Sultanabad, Mahals,

plate **16** | Ziegler Mahal Carpet
West Persia
Last quarter of 19th century
10' x 14'3" (3.05 x 4.34m)
*A rich warm madder-red
background sets the stage for an
array of delicate floral devices
surrounding three central
exaggerated palmettes. The tonal
palette exudes subtle harmony,
and permits one's eye to flow
effortlessly over this lively
carpet. Its fine weave and
lustrous wool yields surface
clarity with a sumptuous patina.*

Zieglers and Farahans all have a cotton foundation, handspun in old examples, and an asymmetric knot.

A large amount of carpets were produced in Sarouk, a village located close to Arak in West-central Persia. The revival of rug production made Sarouk a collecting point for the area's products; as a result, the term Sarouk became a generic term for Arak weavings. Sarouk carpets vary greatly in color, design and structure. Large, strangely shaped medallions covering almost the entire field is a common feature, as are central medallions framed by spandrels.

The Sarouks from 1920-1940 featured an overall design of floral stems and bouquets unattached to each other on a rose ground. During this period, such large amounts were exported to the USA that these carpets were referred to as 'American Sarouks' in the trade. To please the American public, Sarouk carpets were often chemically bleached and tinted with another dye to obtain the desired tone (plates 78, 105). The German market bought many of these 'painted' Sarouks in the last quarter of the 20th century. The name 'Farahan Sarouk' is reserved for the finer pieces of this area, which have velvety short pile (plate 90). The very finest Sarouks are called 'Mahajeran', after an early local manufacturer. These usually have a central medallion on a field of rose or dark red. Yellow guard-stripes flank their wide, midnight-blue borders. Currently,

plate **17** | Mahal Carpet
West Persia
19th century
10' x 14' (3.05 x 4.27m)
*The elegant diamond lattice is
filled with an alternating pattern
which creates rows of similar
cartouches or columns of varying
designs. The simple alternating of
cartouche designs is one that
recurs throughout Persian
carpets.*

Persian Rugs

Sarouks of good quality continue to be made under the label of Jozan, a town that lies in between the Hamadan and Arak regions.

On the fringe of the Great Desert in Central Persia lies Kashan, a city which has a well-documented history of producing extremely fine rugs and textiles. The production is based around city workshops, since the surrounding countryside is an inhospitable desert. The great Ardebil carpets are thought to have been made in Kashan in the 16th century, as well as a group of extremely fine and important silk rugs. It is safe to say that about half of Persia's 19th-century silk rugs were made here, by male craftsmen called 'ustad kar', or master weaver.

In the late 19th century Kashan's traditional craft of making woolen goods collapsed, and the spare wool, a lot of which was merino wool from New Zealand via England, was put to use in reviving rug weaving. A group of rugs made in Kashan at the end of the 19th and the beginning of the 20th centuries featuring elaborate, complex, architectural designs and very fine quality soft wool, is commonly referred to as 'Mohtashem' after the most famous master weaver in the area (plates 26, 96, 98, 111). Good Kashan rugs of this period were also produced under the name 'Dabir.' Nearby Natanz and Haroon are known for a lower grade of rugs. Modern Kashans of 20th century are in light colors and very fine weave (plates 95, 97).

Tehran has been the capital of Persia since 1789 and lies to the East of the Arak region. It has no great tradition of carpet weaving, but the rare examples found today tend to be of fine quality and date from the early to middle of the 20th century. Delicate floral designs incorporating a flowering vase are characteristic and a beautiful shade of rust red sometimes appears.

To the South of Tehran is the city of Veramin. The surrounding area contains a mixture of tribal communities which make tribal rugs and bags, but the city has a more recent tradition of making finer more formal rugs that usually have a the Mina Khani design (plate 40).

Below Arak and Kurdistan, on the Eastern slopes of the Zagros Mountains is another important tribal weaving area, that of the Bakhtiari tribe which inhabits the district of Chahar Mahal and Shahr Kord in the Northeastern fringes of the Zagros Mountains. They have been living in the area since the 16th century and have managed to resist resettlement programs, suffered by the Kurds and other Persian tribes. They were generally much more powerful and prosperous than other tribes in Persia until the authority of their Khans was greatly diminished by Reza Shah in the 1930s and their leaders were exiled to Tehran and even abroad.

The Bakhtiari weaving most familiar in the West is the tile-like pattern often refered to as 'garden design,' however medallion designs can also be found. Old examples, from the middle of the 19th century, have wool foundations but more commonly these carpets are known to have a cotton foundation and symmetric knot; the later the rug, the more likely it is to have a double weft. The nomadic Bakhtiaris weave functional items which mix pile and sumakh, but the majority of the weaving is done in the form of a cottage industry, with a small group of finer workshop-made

plate **18** | Bakhtiari
West Persia
Early 20th century
7' x 10' (2.13 x 3.05m)
A fine Bakhtiari rug of the Zili-sultan pattern which depicts a vase with floral sprays, flanked by a pair of birds. The white ground and generous border help this rug to make a dramatic ensemble.

pieces and Khan carpets made in the urban center of Char Mahal and Faradombeh (plate 77).

To the East of the tribal lands of the Bakhtiari lies the city of Isfahan, the great Safavid capital, and one of the most beautiful cities in Persia. It produced some of the finest Persian carpets in the 16th and 17th centuries (plate 3), including the silk and metal thread Polonaise rugs. In the 1920s, Isfahan reappeared as a rug producer and was once again showing the results of a conscious effort to maintain standard of excellence in its craft. The favorite old themes of central medallions, overall florals, and garden scenes re-emerged in rugs of the high-quality draftsmanship using good wool with silk highlights (plates 19, 99, 101, 102, 103). The workshop of the Serafian, Hekmat Nejad and Rashtian hold the highest reputation of this recent period with highly realistic floral and animal compositions knotted in the finest weave.

Going South toward Kerman is Yazd, which was a notable center of weaving in 17th and 18th century but not too active in 19th and 20th century. An unusual Yazd is illustrated in plate 104.

plate **19** | Isfahan Rug
Central Persia
Circa 1900
4'8" x 6'9" (1.42 x 2.06m)
Overall designs a re the most common of those woven in this city. The pattern here recalls Kerman weaving but the weave and borders, especially the trefoil minors, are pure Isfahan.

Persian Rugs

Southern Persia

In the South and Southwest of Persia are four major tribal groups: in the Province of Fars are the Qashqa'i, the Khamseh confederation, the Lori, and in the Kerman Province, the Afshars. These communities have many different sub-tribes and communities of nomads and settled nomads all of whom have strong tribal identities.

The semi-nomadic Qashqa'i are less numerous than the members of the Khamseh Federation, however, they both market their rugs through the city of Shiraz. Thus, the term Shiraz has come to be used as a label for some generic and less specifically tribal rugs made in the area. Each of the many sub-tribes makes different types of rugs with subtle structural and design details, made on a wool foundation, usually with red wefts and asymmetric wefts.

Taken as a whole, antique Qashqa'i rugs are surely among the finest Persian rugs in terms of wool and dye quality (plate 131). In both of these examples, their ivory border with its hooked angular motifs betrays the Turkish origins of the tribe. A panel at each end of Qashq'ai rugs, composed of three narrow horizontal stripes divided into rectangular compartments and patterned with a white and blue repeat, helps to identify them. The woven and flat-woven saddlebags and kilims are also widely produced by this group closely resembling Beluchi saddlebags in design, with similar stepped polygons in the kilim technique. With tribal tradition rapidly disappearing, these artifacts are becoming more and more difficult to find.

The Khamseh Confederation weaves many different sorts of rugs which reflect the ethnic diversity of its make-up. Many of the designs are similar to those of the Qashq'ai, however Khamseh rugs use mostly dark wool warps, the symmetric knot, and certain border designs. Representation of feeding birds in their rugs are also typical of Khamseh production.

The Loris inhabit the Western reaches of Fars and mix with the Bakhtiari. Their tribal weavings are on a black wool or goat hair foundation and tend to be the loosest of the weavings made by these tribes, rugs with three hooked diamond medallions are commonly ascribed to Loris.

The tribes from Fars, as with many of the other tribal weaving communities of Persia, produced different types of woven products for domestic use. As many of these are woven on a wool foundation, the shape of the rugs is sometimes irregular. These tribes also make gabbehs. These are loosely knotted and coarsely woven rugs that have simple designs and stark color combinations that are admired in the West for their aesthetic boldness and 'modernism' (plates 107, 108).

In the neighboring Province of Kerman, to the North and West of the city of Kerman, live the once powerful Afshar tribe, who were moved by the Safavid monarchy to this area, far from their original homeland located between the Euphrates and Tigris. The best Afshar weaving compare well with the finest tribal rugs from any area in Asia (plates 20, 128, 129, 130). The rugs woven by the Afshars are interesting artistically

plate **20** | AFSHAR RUG
Southeast Persia
19th century
3'7" x 4' (1.09 x 1.22m)
*The rugs woven by the Afshars
are interesting artistically,
because they combine nomadic
individualism with design
influences from the weaving
centers of Kerman. The pile is
wool, and the knots symmetric,
though some instances of
asymmetric knotting may be
found. White or cream colored
wool is also a characteristic
feature of Afshar rugs. The
Afshar tribes have many
different ways of drawing the
boteh, however this is one of the
most characteristics. The deep
blue ground allows the botehs to
float on the field. Notice the
half-design cut off from view by
the borders.*

because they combine nomadic individualism with design influences from the weaving centers of Kerman. Though made by nomads, these rugs often have a foundation of cotton, since the Afshars took them to Kerman for sale and received cotton in exchange. The pile is wool, and the knots symmetric, though some instances of Senneh knot may be found and some are very finely knotted. The design is often composed of diamonds with stylized flowers covering the whole central field, botehs or medallions and four corner designs. Certain border systems and designs are typical of Afshar rugs and can be a simple guide to attribution. The colors are varied and often bright; the ground is usually red or blue or in rare instances white (plates 129, 130).

The city of Kerman is one of the great traditional rug centers of Persia, rugs have been a vital part of the city's trade for a long time. The 19th century revival of the Persian carpet industry allowed for an unprecedented increase in production, many featuring the old Kerman patterns which show graceful floral meanders and birds and animals.

Biblical stories and historical themes were also popular sources of inspiration to the weavers of Kerman who gained fame for their pictorial rugs made around the turn of the last century (plates 27, 110). Throughout the centuries, the Tree of Life design was often used, with its rich arrangement of flowering curvilinear branches and birds (plate 121). This recalls the ancient Persian theme of the walled garden, with its overtones of Paradise. Kerman also produced many medallion-design rugs (plate 21), and extremely rare silk rugs (plate 119). The older pieces are often referred to as 'Laver Kermans', a transformation of the name of the neighboring town of Ravar (plates 79, 110, 112, 113, 114, 115, 116, 117, 119, 120, 124). Blue is commonly used in rugs from the area, particularly since indigo has been cultivated on a vast scale in the region since the 10th century, reds are usually from insect dyes, and they have three wefts in their all cotton foundation. Later Kermans made for the European and American markets, featured lighter shades and pastel colors.

In the Northeastern Khorassan province, the Quchan Kurds, Balouch and Timuri tribes all weave tribal rugs in this region, all of which are avidly collected. The Balouch rugs have a limited color range of blue and red with white used for highlights (plates 201, 202). Khorassan carpets (plate 125) are not common but were in fact, some of the first imported carpets into the West at the beginning of the 19th century. Most of these featured Herati designs, named after the city of Herat which now lies in Afghanistan.

Rug making has revived in this, Persia's poorest region, since the 1880s, with Mashad (plates 75, 109), Dorokhsh (plates 48, 106), Sarakhs, and Mood producing the majority of rugs in this district. Mashad, the capital of Khorassan, is a holy city of shrines, including the shrine of the Imam Ali Reza, with a collection of antique rugs which Cecil Edwards in *The Persian Carpet* describes in detail. A cochineal red appearing as a deep magenta dominates the Mashad rugs. The designs usually follow classical examples of Herati patterns and a paisley originally seen in Kerman shawls from the 16th to 18th centuries. In the 1900s, the Amoghli and Saber workshops of Mashad turned out extraordinary fine rugs for the court of Reza Shah Pahlavi, and later, the Astaneh workshop, still active today, made rugs exclusively for the Imam Reza shrine in Mashad. These rugs occasionally come to market, as they are replaced (plates 75, 109).

plate **21** | Kᴇʀᴍᴀɴ Cᴀʀᴘᴇᴛ
Southeast Persia
19th century
8′5″ x 12′6″ (2.57 x 3.81m)
The elements designed in this carpet are elongated through the larger than average size. The outlining in black allows the design to sit up from the field, as does the differing depth of color in the beautiful rich red ground. The combination of the grand medallion exquisitely constructed color combinations of dark and light shades and, for those that know the irresistibly soft wool, makes this carpet an exceptional weaving.

Persian Rugs

plate **22** | ZIEGLER MAHAL CARPET
Late 19th century
9'10" x 13'10" (3.00 x 4.22m)

*The design of this imposing
carpet is at once sophisticated
and enigmatic, and is a
recognized Ziegler design.
Constructed as a modified prayer
design, its highly unorthodox
use of a linear form creates the
impression of an architectural
structure. At the base lie several
layers of stylized flowers in an
organized symmetrical pattern
that supports a warm madder-
red field. Atop, an indigo portion
comprised of perfectly balanced
floral devices embraces
an ornamental lantern
reminiscent of a classic Ladik
design prayer rug.*

*This classic Ziegler design is
rarely seen on a white ground.
The lancet leaves that flank the
medallion reflect the vivacity
and fluidity of the whole
composition. The multi-layered
nature of the design is clearly
illustrated by the manner in
which the elements scroll above
and below each other. This carpet
has the sophistication associated
with masterpieces created by
Ziegler.*

Persian Rugs

plate **24** | ZIEGLER MAHAL CARPET
West Persia
Circa 1890
9'3" x 17'3" (2.82 x 5.26m)
*This carpet is indicative of
Ziegler production – the area of
ground color that surrounds the
carpet, the multiple guard
stripes, the grass green and other
deeply saturated colors. The
unusual elongated medallion
and pendant design is
complemented by large floral
elements, design components
which can be found on other
Ziegler carpets. The especially
beautiful yet understated border
is a perfect complement to the
ebullient field, highlighting the
complexity of the relationship
between border and field design.*

plate **25** | SULTANABAD CARPET
West Persia
Late 19th century
8′4″ x 12′5″ (2.54 x 3.78m)
This carpet made in the Sultanabad area of Arak province has the well executed open design and saturated colors expected of these beautiful weavings. Note the subtle changes of color used to add detail to the palmettes and arabesques in the designs. It is out of the subtleties such as those seen in this carpet that great textile art is born.

plate **26**

Mohtashem Kashan Carpet
West Persia
Late 19th century
11′5″ x 18′ (3.48 x 5.49m)
*This huge and beautiful rug has
the extremely lustrous wool
typical of Mohtashem rugs. The
lozenge shaped devices in the
field are common in this master
weavers work as are the
flowering plants seen on the
diagonal in the medallion and
repeated in the corners. A
magnificent masterpiece of the
art of weaving.*

plate **27** | Kerman Rug
South Persia
20th century
2'1" x 2'3"

This rug highlights a peculiar product of this weaving area in which feature Christian imagery. Here the Virgin Mary and the infant Jesus are shown on a small-scale rug. Interestingly these rugs, woven by Muslims, were very popular in America at the turn of the century, and many of them seem to have been copied from the same image as is seen by the representation of the crown and halos behind the figures' heads as well as other features. Some people believe that these rugs are the products of the influence of Christian missionaries on the weaving workshop however it seems more likely that they are purely commercial.

plate **28** | Bijar Vagireh
West Persia
20th century
4'11" x 5' (1.50 x 1.52m)

These are pattern samplers made to test patterns or colors. These were given to both weavers and customers to help decide patterns and colorways. They are keenly collected and this piece is of great interest as it charts the design history of this weaving area.

Persian Rugs

plate **29** | Bijar Carpet
West Persia
19th Century
8′9″ x 11′9″ (2.67 x 3.58m)
*This beautiful and colorful Bijar
carpet was made just before
1900 when cotton became used
for the warps. The undecorated
area surrounding the rug, which
reflects the color of the central
field, together with the
exuberant color scheme, are
typical of Bijar weaving. Note
that the intricate design is
multi-layered, as the design
elements that are predominantly
blue create secondary pattern
blocks.*

plate **30** | Silk Bijar Kilim
West Persia
Late 19th century
4′ x 6′6″ (1.22 x 1.98m)
When it comes to rare Kilims,
this extremely fine woven, all
silk Kilim represents the optimal
in design, color and density of a
silk flat woven masterpiece.

Persian Rugs

plate **31** | BIJAR CARPET
West Persia
Late 19th century
6′ x 12′ (1.83 x 3.66m)
*This corridor rug uses the
Persian interpretation of a
European depiction of bouquet
of roses. An interesting element
is that in one of these bouquets
is a small animal put in by the
weaver.*

plate **32**
KURDISH CARPET
Late 19th century
12′ x 14′6″ (3.66 x 4.42m)
*Kurdish rug from the Bakhtiari
region. Very unusual elements
borrowed from many different
Persian weaving areas.*

Persian Rugs

plate **33** | Malayer
Northwest Persia
19th century
4′ x 6′ (1.22 x 1.83m)
This Malayer has a color pallet
of Farahan rugs set on a gold
background with rosettes
spreading over the main field.
The borders are of typical
Farahan or Farahan Sarouk
carpets.

plate **34** | Bijar Rug
West Persia
20th century
3′1″ x 5′5″ (0.94 x 1.65m)
This rug has an all-over design
that has had a medallion
imposed on top of. The usual
form for the corner design is
that of a quarter of the
medallion, however this rug
breaks that tradition. Note that
the white leaves in the herati
design create an ebb and flow
similar to those of waves.

plate **35** | Mahal Carpet
Northwest Persia
Late 19th century
12′ x 20′ (3.66 x 6.10m)
A Herati design rug that has a border of palmettes and leaves typical of these high quality rugs. Seen at a distance, the out-turned leaves that flank the diamond at the heart of the Herati design shaped vine seem to create small medallions.

Persian Rugs

plate **36**
SENNEH AUDIENCE CARPET
West Persia
12′ 11″ x 21′4″ (3.95 x 6.50m)
*Last quarter of the 19th century
One of the rarest examples of
Audience carpets, most possibly
woven for Fatalishah Ghajar or
another ruler of importance.
What sets this example apart is
that the same fine weave of the
smaller carpets has been
employed in a large size. The
Audience carpets are in reality 4
carpets in one, each with a
specific purpose. The top rug
called enthroned is for the King
and his throne. Two carpets on
the two sides for the guards to
stand on and the main carpet for
the audience to walk and kneel
to the throne. The reason there is
no border in the bottom of the
carpet is to remind the audience
that from this point they are at
the presence of the crown and
must proceed accordingly.
The central walkway consists of
the same Herati design flowers
and delicately drawn leaves as
the rest of the carpet, but the
prominence of colors has been
reversed. The three other
sections of the rug contain the
typical rusty color of Senneh
intertwined with light purple,
salmon, olive, taupe, and navy
blue outlines.*

Persian Rugs

plate **37** | SENNEH KILIM
West Persia
Late 19th century
4′6″ x 6′5″ (1.37 x 1.96m)
The soft colors of this extremely
finely woven kilim are
characteristic of the best kilims
from this area. The diamond
medallion and Herati pattern is
common in these kilims but the
botehs borders and guard strips
are unusual.

plate **38** | Bibikabad Carpet
West Persia
20th century
7'3" x 20' (2.21 x 6.10m)
*This carpet is made in a town
Northeast of Hamadan. The
majority of Bibikabad carpets
have boteh or Herati designs,
which makes this particular
example all the more
unusual.*

Persian Rugs

plate **39** | Bijar Runner
West Persia
Circa 1900
4'6" x 11'6" (1.37 x 3.51m)
At the turn of the century
European style flowers,
particularly roses, became a
favorite of Bijar weavers. By the
time that this runner was
woven, the warps of these rugs
had turned from being wool to
machine-spun cotton.

This rug is Kurdish made in the environs of Veramin. The Mina Khani flowers in the border, the brown ground, and the star minor borders are typical of this area.

Persian Rugs

plate **41** | BIJAR CARPET
West Persia
20th century
11′ 7″ x 21′6″ (3.53 x 6.55m)
*This huge carpet represents a
design usually seen on a Heriz
or Serapi carpet. The clever use
of light blue for the ground color
gives a sense of clarity to the
design elements.*

Persian Rugs

plate **42** | BIJAR RUG
West Persia
19th century
4′7″ x 7′5″ (1.40 x 2.26m)
A village rug which the trade used to call Kurd Bijar. It has the triple medallion design that is seen on many secular and tribal rugs.

plate **43**

Northwest Persia
19th century
4' x 9' (1.22 x 2.74m)

*The rug has a design that is of
true Persian origin as it has
enlarged forms of the Herati
design and a flower and
palmette border that is executed
to an equally grand scale. The
dark foundation material and
trefoli minor borders however
point to village production to the
north of the Hamadan region,
quite where though is unclear.*

Persian Rugs

plate **44** | FARAHAN CARPET
West Persia
19th century
14' x 26' (4.25 x 7.90m)

The central field of this massive carpet is a traditional infinite herati design common in rugs from this region, but with the added charm of small birds interspersed throughout. The cream spandrels on both ends of the carpet, with their claw-shaped hooks, create a striking frame and are typical of the region. The black primary border is a version of the famous Zili-Sultan vase-and-flower motif with the addition of the decorative birds. Enlargements have been reproduced in the spandrels. The colors in the carpet have been employed with great artistry and are quite varied.

Persian Rugs

plate **46** | Mɪsʜᴀɴ Mᴀʟᴀʏᴇʀ Rᴜɢ
Northwest Persia
Circa 1900
4′ 4″ x 6′6″ (1.32 x 1.98m)

*This Mishan Malayer is the best
of the Malayer rugs. The white
ground and beautifully open
field are features that many
collectors look for in these rugs.
The grandeur of the field design
is augmented by small and
delicate borders to make a truly
stunning rug.*

plate **48** | Dorokhsh Carpet
Northeast Persia
20th century
10'4" x 17' (3.15 x 5.18m)
*Doroksh carpets from the
mountainous Qainat region are
rare, and this example is
particularly unusual as many
have very small intricate
designs. Flowering shrubs
accompany the elongated Herati
design. It is equally unusual to
see three main borders of the
same size as we do here. The
depth of color and spaciousness
of the design make for an
elegant carpet.*

Persian Rugs

plate **49** | Malayer Rug
West Persia
3'5" x 5'2" (1.04 x 1.57m)
*A village type of rug. The people
and animals in the white
ground, or what could represent
the desert, add a touch of humor
to the rug, something that one
finds in many provincial and
informal rugs. The lack of a
clearly defined inner guard
between the main border and
ground is uncommon.*

plate **50** | Tᴀʙʀɪᴢ Rᴜɢ
Northwest Persia
19th century
9′8″ x 13′4″ (2.95 x 4.06m)
*This excellent Hajji Jalili carpet
has the intricacy of design and
subtle variety of color that are
distinctive to these carpets. The
light blue, tan and oatmeal
colors are eminently popular in
today's interior design market.
The grading of the changing
colors produces a depth of color
and design that creates many
different layers to the design.
The beauty of the carpet as a
whole is reflected in that of its
individual elements.*

Pᴇʀsɪᴀɴ Rᴜɢs

plate **51** | Tᴀʙʀɪᴢ Rᴜɢ
Northwest Persia
19th century
3′9″ x 5′4″ (1.14 x 1.63m)
This rug of the Hajji Jalili type typifies the colors of the genre. The ivory ground of the field suggests that the medallion and pendants are floating in space.

plate **52** | Tabriz Rug
Northwest Persia
19th century
4'7" x 6'4" (1.40 x 1.93m)
*The light color of this rug makes
it a highly desirable item in the
decorative market. The details
and outline in light and dark
blue complement the subtle
colors. This medallion is unusual
and mixes botehs, drawn as they
are usually found in shawls,
with sprays of blossoms.*

Persian Rugs

plate **53** | Tabriz Carpet
Northwest Persia
19th century
9'7" x 13' (2.92 x 3.96m)

*This Hajji Jalili Tabriz shows the
work of this esteemed master
craftsman. The exquisite
scrolling vines within the
spandrel and medallion give rise
to the palmettes and pendants
that float in the rich butterscotch
ground. The clarity of the center
of the medallion adds a serenity
to the complexity of the rest of
the field. The borders are as
beautifully rendered as the field,
the cartouches echoing the
design inside the medallion. The
border corner designs highlight
the expertise of the designer.*

plate **54** | Tabriz Carpet
Northwest Persia
20th century
8'5" x 11' (2.57 x 3.35m)
*The vase design is executed with
the characteristic aplomb of the
Tabriz weavers. The design is
called 'vase' after a group of
Safavid rugs that have these
symmetric design of flowerheads
that issued from a vase which
was sometimes seen at the
bottom of the field and
sometimes not.*

Persian Rugs

plate **55** | Heriz Carpet
Northwest Persia
Late 19th century
4'6" x 6'4"
*Small rugs from this period of
production in the region is quite
uncommon, as most of the rugs
made there were meant for
export to foreign markets where
room size rugs were in demand.
This rug does however show that
the small sizes used a scaled
down version of elements used
in the larger weavings.*

plate **56** | BAKHSHAISH CARPET
Northwest Persia
Circa 1900
9′ 2″ x 13′ (2.80 x 3.96m)

This rug is atypical in its use of an all-over field design. At first glance, it looks indiscriminate, but upon closer examination, one finds a well thought-out design with particular attention paid to placement of the floral bouquets. The trellis surrounding the flowers is reminiscent of a formal garden.

Persian Rugs

plate **57** | HERIZ CARPET
Northwest Persia
20th century
11'8" x 14'5" (3.56 x 4.39m)
*This 20th century
reinterpretation of an antique
Serapi design, paying attention
to the details, makes this rug an
excellent copy.*

plate **58** | Serapi Carpet
Northwest Persia
Late 19th century
9′8″ x 12′5″ (2.95 x 3.78m)

The size of the medallion has dictated that the borders need to be of a lesser scale to create the harmony necessary in all great carpet and textile art. The layout of the field creates a layered effect, which, through the subtle use of color shading, allows the white central medallion to look as though it is sitting on a layer below the rest of the carpet.

Persian Rugs

plate **59** | Serapi Carpet
19th century
12'5" x 23' (3.80 x 7.00m)

This magnificent palatial rug is elegant in its simplicity and soothing, rich color tones. The quality of wool and fineness of weave is extraordinary. The scale of the carpet impresses and makes some of the simple individual elements items of great abstract art. The different depths of color in the red and light blue, called abrash, transmit depth to the design. The calligraphy in the unusual guard border is poems from the famous Persian poet, Hafiz.

Persian Rugs

plate **60** | SERAPI CARPET
Northwest Persia
19th century
8′9″ x 12′7″ (2.62 x 3.84m)
*This Serapi carpet has the
depressed warps and grand scale
of the best Serapis. The grand
scale of the medallion and the
clarity of color show that this
carpet would make a bold
statement in any room. The
yellow details in the center of
the medallion lead the eye to the
medallion and then out to its
edges. This carpet has been
created straight from the
weaver's memory rather than a
cartoon, lending it a certain
charming, almost naïve vitality.
A delicate and spacious border
complements the strength of the
field design. The deep indigo
gives the medallion a three
dimensional quality.*

plate **61** | SERAPI RUG
Northwest Persia
19th century
5′2″ x 6′7″ (1.57 x 2.01m)
Small Serapi rugs are rare and
this beautiful little rug has the
fine coloring and clear design of
many Serapi carpets. The tracery
surrounding the medallion in
two shades of light blue
highlight the layered effect that
this medallion presents. The
tracery in the white spandrels in
the corners of the field is
particularly finely drawn. A rug
that deserves to be looked at for
a while.

Persian Rugs

plate **62** | Serapi Carpet
Northwest Persia
19th century
6′3″ x 9′ (1.91 x 2.74m)
A spacious medallion design
carpet of fine weave. The detail
of the design is particularly well
executed through the clever use
of white which creates a depth to
the design.

plate **63** | Bibikabad
8′5″ x 11′8″ (2.57 x 3.56m)
*Hamadan area is home for
production of these single wafted
rugs, normally in large sizes. In
this particular example, a
Bakhshaish design is executed
with great precision.*

plate **64** | Karadja Carpet
Northwest Persia
Mid 19th century
10'2" x 16'7" (3.10 x 5.05m)
*This carpet has an unusual
variant of the harshang design,
which is usually seen on many
old carpets made in Azerbaijan
and the Caucasus. The
spaciousness of the drawing and
the flaming nature of the
palmettes show that this is part
of an earlier generation of
carpet, as do the yellow minor
borders. Carpets of this age and
shape were made for important
houses in Azerbaijan to be
placed in the gallery of the
house where guests would see it.
This carpet is both decorative
and collectable.*

plate **65** | KARADJA RUNNER
Northwest Persia
19th century
3′5″ x 14′7″ (1.04 x 4.45m)
*This thick runner is finely made
and has the strong trefoil outer
border and white ground
meandering vine middle border
common on this group.*

plate **66** | SARAB RUNNER
Northwest Persia
19th century
3′5″ x 12′8″ (1.04 x 3.86m)
*A beautiful example of a Sarab
runner that has the
characteristic frame of camel-
colored ground and column of
medallions in the field. The small
elements filling the field and
border are especially beautifully
drawn.*

Persian Rugs

plate **67** | Heriz Carpet
Northwest Persia
20th century
10′8″ x 21′7″ (3.25 x 6.55m)
*This modern carpet shows that
beautiful carpet is still being
made in Northwest Persia using
traditional techniques, designs
and colors.*

plate **68**
BAKHSHAISH DESIGN CARPET
Northwest Persia
20th century
16' x 18'7" (4.88 x 5.66m)
This modern carpet confidently
continues the tradition of the
late 19th century village
weavings.

Persian Rugs

plate **70** | Bakhshaish Carpet
Northwest Persia
19th century
11′8″ x 15′2″ (3.56 x 4.62m)
*This multi-layered design shows
the height of the weaving art in
the Heriz area carpets. The
decoration inside the medallion
is typical of Bakhshaish carpets,
as is the deeply abrashed blue
ground. It is interesting to note
that the blue ground is revealed
once more in the medallion, an
indication that the design should
be seen in terms of layers.*

Persian Rugs

plate **72** | Bijar Runner
West Persia
Circa 1900
4′5″ x 11′3″ (1.35 x 3.43m)
This runner has the unusual feature of a pendant medallion design and a camel-colored ground. The design is reminiscent of Senneh rugs but the weave portrays the thick weave of a Bijar rug.

plate **73** | Kurdish Mat
3′5″ x 4′8″ (1.04 x 1.42m)
This is typical example of flat woven prayer mats that Kurdish people of Sanandadj – Iran wove mostly for their own use with natural colors of black – white and brown. The similarity of these colors and design to Navaho rugs is subject of research by the author.

plate **74**
NORTHWEST PERSIAN RUNNER
19th century
3'10" x 20'3" (1.17 x 6.17m)
This carpet has all the characteristics of a Kurdish rug from the village of Sauj Bulak including the red wefts. The colors are as exuberant as one would expect and the border is an interpretation of a border found on early 19th century northwest Persian carpets. As is the case in many carpets from this village, a standard Persian design is transformed into a veritable enigma.

Persian Rugs

plate **76** | Kʀᴅɪsʜ Rᴜɴɴᴇʀ
Northwest Persia
19th century
3'7" x 16'9" (1.09 x 5.11m)
*The brown outside border is
unusual, but the field
incorporates elements from
northwest Persian and West
Persian rugs. As with many
Kurdish weavings, the dyes and
color palette are excellent.*

plate **75** | Mashad Runner;
Signed Astaneh
Northeast Persia
20th century
3'5" x 16' (1.04 x 4.88m)
*The rich dyes and single border
create a singularly attractive
and bold composition.*

Persian Rugs

plate 77 | Bakhtiari Carpet
West Persia
19th century
15' x 24' (4.57 x 7.32m)
This huge Bakhtiari carpet was made for one of the Bakhtiari Khans. A translation of the inscription cartouche in the top border reads, Made for His Excellency Ali Akbar Khan Bakhtiari, in 1303 – this relates to 1885 in the Roman calendar. These Khan carpets are rare and important, and have been the subject of much academic research. The pattern is a variant of the herati design which is intricately drawn, however, this is offset by the white ground which imparts a certain rhythm to the design. Note that the bottom border and field become somewhat squashed as the end of the rug is reached by the weavers. The complex major border is a rare, perhaps unique, interpretation of a 17th century strapwork border. A masterpiece of draftsmanship which has all the charm of a tribal weaving.

plate **78** | Sᴀʀᴏᴜᴋ Cᴀʀᴘᴇᴛ
West Persia
20th century
10′8″ x 15′ (3.23 x 4.57m)
*A so called American Sarouk,
this displays the color that the
American market demanded in
the early 20th century. The red
ground is scattered with
flowering trees and centered by
a vase in the middle of this bilateral design field.*

Pᴇʀsɪᴀɴ Rᴜɢs

plate **79**
RAVAR KERMAN CARPET
Southeast Persia
Circa 1860
8'6" x 16'10" (2.59 x 5.13m)
This gallery size carpet has been influenced by European pictures of roses. The gul faranghi, meaning literally foreign flowers, is reflected in the interpretation of the zili-sultan border. Identical to a rug of same proportion in the Cairo museum.

plate **80** | Bakhtiari
3′7″ x 5′ (1.09 x 1.52m)
*A great example of tribal
weaving of Bakhtiari area.*

plate **81** | Farahan Hall Rug
West Persia
5'6" x 13' (1.68 x 3.96m)

This carpet feature a crowded herati field framed by an unusual border of tree motifs enclosed by diamond. The design is drawn with certain sophistication and precision, however it is curious that the weaver decided to include a primitive boteh in each corner which reminds people of the tribal origins of the design.

plate **82** | Malayer Carpet
Northwest Persia
19th century
13'2" x 24'6" (4.01 x 7.47m)
*This unusually large Malayer
carpet combines the soft pinky
red, light blue and white of the
best Malayers into a
harmonious composition. The
design is two-way as the bird
sitting in the delicately rendered
floral sprays can be seen to the
right way up from both ends of
the carpet.*

Persian Rugs

plate **83** | FARAHAN CARPET
West Persia
19th century
10 '4" x 20'4" (3.15 x 6.20m)
The central field of this carpet is
a traditional Herati design that
often appears in rugs from this
region. When examined from
afar, a diamond lattice emerges
from the juxtapositions of the
herati. The primary border of
arabesques is surrounded by
guard border stripes of small
flowers and botehs.

plate **84** | S<small>ULTANABAD</small> C<small>ARPET</small>
West Persia
Late 19th century
13'6" x 22'10" (4.11 x 6.35m)
*The strapwork border is derived
from 16th century Safavid
carpets, and is drawn with a
characteristic precision here. The
small lobed medallion design is
not situated in the middle of the
carpet, which suggests that this
carpet was designed to be viewed
from one end, thus creating the
illusion of symmetry in the
design.*

Persian Rugs

plate **85** | Sᴜʟᴛᴀɴᴀʙᴀᴅ Cᴀʀᴘᴇᴛ
West Persia
5'3" x 10' (1.60 x 3.05m)
*The white ground and clearly
articulated field design make this
carpet a very desirable rug in
the decorative market, in which
high prices are keenly paid for
such items. The palmette border,
which has unusually short arms
extending from its sides,
surrounding a complex trellis
containing henna flowers is
often used in rugs from this
area.*

*This Mahal uses a design that is
particular to the Arak weaving
area. The henna flowers are
larger than one usually sees and
the border is precisely drawn to
counterbalance the field
composition.*

plate **88** | MAHAL CARPET
West Persia
Early 20th century
9' 8" x 13' (2.95 x 3.96m)

*Lobed cartouches are created by
the movement of the feathered
vine in the richly decorated
madder ground. The delicate
flow of the field is not impeded
by the relative simplicity of the
borders.*

*The coloring of this carpet is
typical of the Mahal weavings of
the late 19th and early 20th
centuries.*

Persian Rugs

plate **89** | Mahal Carpet
West Persia
20th century
10′6″ x 18′6″ (3.20 x 5.64m)
*The light rose colored field
provides a subtle backdrop for
the meandering vine and
arabesque pattern that
incorporates some of the
building blocks of the Herati
pattern. The design is made up
by three vertical bands, the two
outer ones being similar.*

plate **90** | Sᴀʀᴏᴜᴋ Cᴀʀᴘᴇᴛ
West Persia
20th century
8′ x 9′6″ (2.44 x 2.90m)
An unusual medallion designed
Sarouk. Great color harmony.

Persian Rugs

plate **92** | Mahal Carpet
West Persia
19th century
10′5″ x 14′ (3.18 x 4.27m)
*An attractive all-over design
which has the distinctive green
and madder colors of the Mahal
rugs. The flower heads are not
perfectly rounded which adds to
their charm.*

Persian Rugs

plate **93** | Sᴜʟᴛᴀɴᴀʙᴀᴅ Cᴀʀᴘᴇᴛ
West Persia
19th century
14'5" x 28'7" (4.39 x 8.71m)
*The palatial proportions of this
carpet are more than adequately
matched by the superbly athletic
design of scrolling vines issuing
flowerheads. The complexity of
the design is created through the
use of various different shades
in the vinery so that a liquidity
is given to the pattern units. The
border is more common on
weavings from Joshaghan.*

Persian Rugs

plate **94** | Mahal Carpet
Northwest Persia
Late 19th century
6'8" x 10'4" (2.06 x 2.30m)
*This scrolling floral bouquet
design is called the Mustofi
design and is common in these
Arak weavings.*

plate **95** | KASHAN CARPET
Central Persia
20th century
11′ x 14′ (3.35 x 4.25m)
The two plane design gives a
tile-like effect to this carpet. The
diamond lattice is punctuated by
small rosettes which are
repeated in the border, creating a
certain symmetry.

Persian Rugs

plate **96**
MOHTASHEM KASHAN RUG
Central Persia
Early 20th century
4'6" x 6'7" (1.37 x 2.01m)
This Mohtashem rug is divided
though the field and medallion
through the use of a lattice
interspersed with lozenges
containing flowers. The
cockscomb motifs are typical of
this master weaver's work, as
are the beautifully rendered
flowers and petals and deep blue
ground. The border reflects the
lattice design of the field.

plate **97** | Kᴀꜱʜᴀɴ Cᴀʀᴘᴇᴛ
Central Persia
20th century
10′5″ x 18′3″ (3.16 x 5.56m)
A fine woven example featuring
a pattern of floral bouquets
borrowed from antique Kerman
carpets.

plate **98** | KASHAN CARPET
20th century
4′ x 6′4″ (1.22 x 1.93m)
*Combining vase design and bird
of Paradise design this very fine
rug is typical of work produced
by the Dabir workshop in
Kashan.*

plate **99** | Isfahan Carpet
Central Persia
20th century
10′9″ x 14′4″ (3.28 x 4.37m)
*This carpet exemplifies the
height that Isfahan weaving
achieved in the 20th century. The
fineness of the weave is matched
by the intricacy of the design.
Although a relatively modern
weaving, the four and one
medallion design is one that
recurs throughout the history of
carpet weaving.*

Persian Rugs

plate **100** | Silk and
Metal Thread Farahan Rug
20th century
4'4" x 6'9" (1.32 x 2.06m)
*These metal thread and raised
pile rugs are called souf. They
use the same techniques as those
employed for the famous 17th
century Polonaise carpets.
Farahan souf are rare, but their
colors are the perfect vehicle for
this medium.*

plate **101** | Isfahan Rug
Central Persia
Circa 1900
4′7″ x 7′6″ (1.40 x 2.29m)
A beautiful stylized prayer rug design showing the weavers' skill in depicting animals and birds. Note the texture and depth given to the flowers through the painterly use of shading.

Persian Rugs

plate **102** | Isfahan Carpet
Central Persia
20th century
13′9″ x 20′8″ (4.19 x 6.30m)
An exceptionally fine large
Isfahan carpet. The majority of
the Isfahan carpets of this
quality are in inportant private
collections.

plate **103** | Isfahan Carpet
Central Persia
20th century
10'4" x 13'6" (3.15 x 4.11m)
An exceptionally large, fine and beautiful Isfahan carpet that exhibits the skill of both the designer and weaver to create this degree of complexity. Note the lavish unfurling of the medallion's layers.

plate **104** | Yazd Carpet
Northeast Persia
20th century
13′ x 19′ (3.96 x 5.79m)
*A beautiful large trefoil design
that appears in the positive and
negative spaces of the field to
create an all-over design that
has simplicity and complexity,
curvilinear and rectilinear
elements.*

plate **105** | Sarouk Carpet
West Persia
20th century
10′ x 12′9″ (3.05 x 3.89m)
*This colorful carpet is typical of
20th century Sarouk design that
uses strong colors and large yet
intricate designs of roses and
other flowers to create a
harmonious whole.*

Persian Rugs

plate **106** | Dorokhsh Carpet
Northeast Persia
19th century
16' x 19' (4.88 x 5.79m)
*The ubiquitous Herati design is
used with small rosettes with
white details which add a
different twist to this design. The
abrashed blue ground border
greatly enhances the field of the
rug and acts as an ideal frame.*

plate **107** | Gabbeh Rug
Southeast Persia
20th century
5′ x 6′5″ (1.52 x 1.96m)
*A typically bold and simple
design for a simple functional
tribal weaving.*

plate **108** | Gabbeh Rug
Northeast Persia
20th century
3' x 6' (0.91 x 1.83m)
*This gabbeh is made not by the
nomads of the Fars region as one
may expect but, rather in fact in
the Kurdish villages North of
Mashad. The rug's attractiveness
lies in its simplicity.*

plate **109**

MASHAD CARPET; SIGNED SABER
Northeast Persia
20th century
13' x 19' (3.96 x 5.79m)
*This modern Mashad has two of
the features that are most
sought after in the market: a
white ground and an all-over
design. The design is perfectly
symmetrical along the central
axis.*

Persian Rugs

plate **III** | Dᴀʙɪʀ Kᴀꜱʜᴀɴ
11'8″ x 17′ (3.56 x 5.18m)
*A wonderful example from this
famed workshop with
reinterpreted Joshegan design
woven with such a precision and
the best of material.*

plate **112** | Ravar Kerman Rug
Southeast Persia
19th century
4′8″ x 5′10″ (1.42 x 1.78m)
*The layout of this rug is very
unusual. The field is a section
from a much larger design that
has been blown up so that it
uses the whole ground. The large
trefoil design in the middle of
the field is reflects the design of
the mihrab.*

plate **113** | RAVAR KERMAN
4'3" x 6'3" (1.30 x 1.91m)
This classic Ravar Kerman is a great representation of the 19th artists who created many wonderful examples.

plate **114**
RAVAR KERMAN CARPET
Southeast Persia
Late 19th century
8'10" x 12'2" (2.62 x 3.68m)
*The dense foliate ground
supports a series of medallions
that frame a deep indigo ground
border. Note the swirling motion
of the floral ground in the
central medallion. The use of a
medallion that is repeated only
along the central horizontal axis
is unusual.*

plate **115** | Ravar Kerman Carpet
Southeast Persia
19th century
9′ x 12′8″ (2.74 x 3.89m)
*The design has all the
characteristics of the Baroque
style of Kerman carpets through
its use of boteh design and the
swirling lozenges and lobed
medallion.*

Persian Rugs

plate **116** | Ravar Kerman
Southeast Persia
Mid 19th century
18′ x 28′ (5.49 x 8.53m)
This oversized carpet symbolizes the skill of the carpet designers of Kerman and Persia in general. The pattern works on two levels, that of a profusion of detailed flowers and also on a grand scale showing a selected view of a continuing repeat of a medallion design. The borders contain poems with Kufic insertion which echo the beauty of the field that they frame.

Persian Rugs

plate **117** | Ravar Kerman Rug
Southeast Persia
19th century
4'6" x 6'9" (1.37 x 2.06m)
This design is usually seen on a group of Farahan rugs and carpets. However, here the weavers of the village of Ravar have executed it with their characteristic colors and minor borders. The drawing of the flowers in the field is particularly beautiful.

plate **118** | Kerman Saddle Rug
Southeast Persia
Late 19th century
3'8" x 4' (1.12 x 1.22m)
These unusual rugs, made to be used to be over a saddle, are usually made for ceremonial or prestigious purposes rather than actual used often, since this would wear them considerably. However if used they would impart great status to the owner. These are eagerly sought after by collectors. Saddle rugs of Farahan and Senneh are more common.

Persian Rugs

plate **119**
SILK RAVAR KERMAN RUG
Southeast Persia
19th century
4′6″ x 6′5″ (.37 x 1.96m)
Silk Ravar Kermans are very
rare and the crispness of the
design and weaving make this
an excellent example of its rare
type. Great care has been taken
over choosing the colors for this
rug, and the subtlety of the
floral designs is almost
unbelievable. The elegant
contours of the mihrab show
that this is a prayer design. The
borders are particularly
beautiful. The signiture is that of
the famous master workshop of
Sadeghiani.

plate **120** | Ravar Kerman
Southeast Persia
Late 19th century
9′ x 12′ (2.74 x 3.66m)
*The light color with accents of
the pattern detailed by the use of
deep crimson adds subtlety to
this magnificent carpet that is
hard to surpass. The border and
field are perfect balanced in their
design and coloring.*

Persian Rugs

plate **121** | Kerman Carpet
Southeast Persia
Late 19th century
9′ x 12′ (2.74 x 3.66m)
*This view of Paradise sees the
garden and kiosks that are part
of the formal gardens of the
Safavids. These gardens were
actually built and depicted in
their contemporary weavings.
The addition of peacocks is also
seen in the great Safavid carpets
of the 16th century, as are the
animal combatants seen in the
spandrels.*

plate **122** | Kᴇʀᴍᴀɴ Rᴜɢ
Southeast Persia
19th century
4'5" x 7' (1.35 x 2.13m)
*This beautifully colored rug has
the light blue and crimson lac
red color that epitomize Kerman
rugs. The design is an interesting
mixture of both textile and
carpet motifs which have been
combined to create a free-
flowing open pattern.*

Persian Rugs

plate **124**

RAVAR KERMAN CARPET
Southeast Persia
Late 19th century
13′6″ x 20′7″ (4.11 x 6.27m)
This densely woven and pattern carpet cleverly combines both curvilinear and geometric motives to great affect. The use of different color combinations in the medallions in the field, all of which contain the same motifs, demonstrates the skill of the designer in creating a texture to the regularity of the design.

plate **125** | Khorassan Carpet
Northeast Persia
Late 19th century
6'6" x 20'5" (1.98 x 6.22m)
*This gallery carpet has a design
that is intricate but drawn with
such vivacity and space that its
three individual elements are a
treat to the eye. An interpreted
and beautiful Kerman design,
probably a special commission.*

plate **126** | SɪʀJAN Soғʀᴇʜ
Southwest Persia
20th century
4'9" x 4'9" (1.45 x 1.45m)
This product of the tribes found to the South of Kerman is flatwoven and was originaly made to wrap bread in to keep it fresh. The beautiful and clear design is indicative of great minimalist art and the design repertoire of the tribes of Southern Persia.

Persian Rugs

plate **127** | Sɪʀᴊᴀɴ Sᴏғʀᴇʜ
Southwest Persia
20th century
5'2" x 5' (1.57 x 1.52m)
This simply design bread sofreh worked in sumakh and flatweave makes a bold and graphic statement.

plate **128** | AFSHAR RUG
Southeast Persia
19th century
6'2" x 13'7" (1.88 x 4.14m)
This cane design is popular in
South Persian rugs, known as
Mohremati design after
Mohremati shawls. The stripes of
the cane design, which look as
though they are minor borders,
appear in a field that is imposed
upon another field design of
small botehs. The exuberance of
the design components and the
fun of the unexpected
composition are part of the
idiosyncratic nature of these
weavings.

Persian Rugs

plate **130** | Afshar Rug
Southeast Persia
Circa 1900
4′6″ x 5′10″ (1.37 x 1.78m)
The zigzag design of stripes outlining the medallions produces a brilliant eye-dazzling effect. The hooked medallions and bird-shaped forms in the outer white ground border are characteristic of Afshar rugs.

Persian Rugs

plate **131** | Qashqa'i Rug
Southwest Persia
20th century
5' x 8'7" (1.52 x 2.54m)
*This prayer rug design is called
the millefleurs design. There is a
group of Indian prayer rugs of
this type dating from the 16th
century to the present day. There
is also a group of finely made
Qashqa'i millfleurs rugs to
which this is an important
addition.*

Turkish Rugs

The heritage of Turkey is intertwined so closely to its history of carpet and textile weaving that the two cannot be studied separately. Research of the full spectra of Turkish carpet history requires and deserves an entire book of its own, hence we are concentrating this study to the weaving from the 16th century on.

Geographic location at once explains the variety of influences on Turkish rug art: Persia, Armenia and the Caucasus on the East, and Europe and Egypt to the West, by sea. The Anatolian peninsula, the Asian part of Turkey, is surrounded by the Aegean, Mediterranean Oceans, the Black Sea and the Sea of Marmara. It is hardly surprising that Turkish rugs were exported to Europe from the 16th century onwards. The ports of Izmir and Istanbul exported Ottoman and Turkish culture throughput the globe. In the 17th century, Turkish exports were so prevalent that any Oriental rug was called a Turkey carpet, and these were imitated in England by using a method called 'turkeywork'. Turkish rugs were seen as symbols of luxury and thus appear in many European paintings of the 16th century as symbols of wealth. Turkish weavers incorporated elements of design from the severe rectilinear grid-work of early Seljuk rugs to the curvilinear elegance of classical Persian pieces. The areas surrounding these ports have been weaving areas for hundreds of years, in the 17th and 18th centuries, small format, prayer format, and Ottoman court style were the mainstay of the made for export weaving. The 19th century brought an increase in large room-sized carpets, just as it did in Persia.

This high and arid Anatolian plateau is most mountainous in the East, where Mt. Ararat rises over 18,000 feet, an ideal environment for raising sheep.

Traditional Turkish rugs are made from native wool, which varied greatly in quality and, until the 19th century, rugs were woven almost entirely from this material. However throughout Anatolia, peasant women bred their own silkworms, which provided the silk for districts like Bursa to produce silk rugs (plate 132). The nomadic tribes, including the great number of Kurds in Southeast Anatolia, favored goat hair, which can still be seen in the high-pile symmetric knot Yuruk rugs.

The wool was dyed with many of the standard natural dyes: madder and citric acids for making their rusts and vermilion; golden yellow came primarily from acorns and lye residue, and light yellow from a lemon base; the characteristic green was derived from the hait plant and copper sulfate; black from a delicate mixture of volcanic muds.

In the 19th century, countless rugs were produced for European export. They ranged in quality from the finest Hereke silks to the most barbarized, loosely woven rugs with the poorest quality aniline dyes, following designs dictated by the foreign markets. For centuries, the Greek and Armenian communities wove the finest pieces, with Armenian inscriptions suggesting that the involvement of Armenians in Turkic carpet weaving was quite extensive, especially during the 16th and 17th centuries. The Christian Greeks lived in parts of Anatolia from the first millennium B.C., and their population was tolerated by the Ottomans until World War I. Throughout Turkey, thousands of peasants still pursue weaving for additional income, therefore the Turkish carpet industry has two distinct, and different products; one made in workshops, the other by a cottage industry or rural community.

plate **132** | Bursa Silk
4'3" x 6'3" (1.30 x 1.91m)
Doubled prayer design of this Bursa silk rug with unusual architectural elements and hanging lamps represents the innovative skills of Bursa weavers.

The prayer rug represents one of the most expressive of Turkish woven forms. Five times a day, the devout kneels on his rug with the arch directed toward Mecca and places a pilgrimage stone at its point. Most prayer rugs have a representation of a mihrab, the part of the mosque which orientates the pious towards Mecca and the sacred Ka'ba, which symbolizes man's relationship with God and the path of submission to His will. This path ultimately leads to a heavenly paradise, often depicted in prayer rugs by beautiful floral and leaf designs or the Tree of Life. Many prayer rugs also depict a hanging mosque lamp representing the light of God, a symbolic use of light shared with Judaism and Christianity. Birds, representing the human soul, are a recurring theme, while the phoenix and

Turkish Rugs

dragon symbols borrowed from China and shared with Christianity, appear in many stylized forms to signify the struggle between good and evil.

Particularly in Anatolian prayer rugs architectural designs occur but these themes differ in other rugs as this reflects the geographic and cultural diversity of Islam. 17th century Ghiordes examples of the tripartite arch recalls those of the Roman Empire. The products of many of the towns below include prayer rugs but they may not be mentioned specifically.

In the Istanbul District is Hereke where in 1884, the Sultan Abdul Mejid established royal carpet factory in the old textile weaving center and commissioned Persian master-weavers to set up the highest quality weaving industry. This resulted in rugs woven entirely of silk, with more than one million knots per square yard (plate 156). The silk Hereke testifies to the heights reached in formal designs, betraying Persian inspiration in elegant oval medallions and gracefully cloud bands and floral sprays. Istanbul itself has the famous Kum Kapi workshops which produces Persian inspired silk and metal thread prayer rugs of exquisite fineness made in Armenian workshops.

Almost ninety percent of all Turkish rugs are produced in Anatolia, the Asian portion of what is now Turkey, and many good books have been exclusively devoted to Anatolian carpets. The small Anatolian towns of Ghiordes and Kula, West of Ushak and Southwest of Ankara, have earned a high regard for their magnificent prayer rugs. Ghiordes produced primarily prayer rugs in the 18th and 19th centuries, many of which found their way into Western collections. The small size beautiful Ghiordes prayers rugs were popular in 18th century (plates 153, 154). Rugs from this town usually measure less than seven feet, and come in cool color schemes, but medallion patterns were made in addition to prayer-rug designs. In rare cases, room size Ghiordes rugs were made with center medallion or enlarged prayer design. These were usually made for important customers on a per-order basis (plate 136). The silver-gray and heliotrope are again typical of subdued Ghiordes colors. An interesting example that has a cool color scheme, with the traditional prayer arch and floral bouquet suspended over a pale pistachio mihrab is featured in plate 151. The 'Kiz Ghiordes' appear in a small, squarish format of a medallion rug with a broad wavy band in the border. These are thought to have been a traditional dowry piece. Later rugs were produced with cotton wefts and cotton as pile highlights. The design of Ghiordes prayer rugs were copied throughout Anatolia, in Panderma mercerized cotton was used as pile to give the same luster as silk.

Kula rugs frequently have multiple border stripes, usually seven, often featuring the *Shobokli*, or pipe-stem, pattern, and a horizontal panel above the mihrab, as opposed to two in Ghiordes rugs. Columns are characteristic of the earlier rugs. A characteristic Kula design called *mezarlik*, (cemetery) depicts small repeating arrangements of a house flanked by two cypresses, usually on a dark field. They have been found in tombs, hence their name.

Just East of these towns is Ushak, located roughly 100 miles directly South of Istanbul. This is a prolific weaving area. The distinctive design of the carpets from this city appear as early as the 15th century in the paintings of Lorenzo Lotto and they are mentioned as part of the booty of the Polish king, John III Sobieski.

One of the most popular designs woven in the Ushak region from the 16th century onwards is that of the medallion Ushak. These rugs constitute one of the largest and earliest groups of Turkish carpets exported to the West. They make a one of the largest groups of extant weavings from this period anywhere. Many of the large houses in Europe used these carpets to decorate tables and they appear in numerous paintings of the period. The manner in which they appear show that they are seen to be items that confered status on the people in the portraits and were objects of great value. There are many variants within this group, however many of the best examples do have various characteristics in common. These are the red ground with a dense and finely drawn in blue floral tracery (plate 133).

The large-scale medallion carpets of the 17th century exemplify the weaving of this area and that of the Ottoman court (plate 138). In the 19th century, the traditional deep indigo and vermilion tones of the so-called 'Star Ushak' gave way to more subtle earth tones of coral, ivory, gray, and olive green (plates 143, 144, 145). These large rugs also lent themselves to the export trade, thus this area in West Anatolia was responsible for many

plate **133** | Ushak Carpet
19th century
6'9" x 11'2" (2.06 x 3.40m)
The rich, deep color of this carpet is found on the medallion Ushak carpets of the 16/17th centuries. The abrash of the medallion creates a feeling of infinite depth to the central motif.

Turkish Rugs

of the large rugs made in the 19th century to furnish Western homes. The large carpets, sometimes called Smyrna or just Turkey carpets, typically had blood red grounds and all-over patterns derived from the weaving repertoire of Ushak carpets of previous centuries. The tradition of export weavings continued, however, as is the case with many increases in weaving production throughout history, the quality suffered by the early 20th century. Many of the Ushak carpets seen today date from the period of the late 19th century when these rugs were being made for the large department stores in the West, which would have their label sewn and sometimes woven into the back of the rug. The difference between Ushak, Sparta, and Ghiordes rugs, all of which bear similar designs and were woven to satisfy the Western room-size decorative market, is that Ushak carpets use the asymmetric knot on a wool foundation, whereas Ghiordes rugs have a cotton foundation and Sparta rugs use an asymmetric knot.

Overall design Ushaks combining geometric designs with interconnecting floral arrangements are a group of rugs currently in high demand (plates 137, 140, 145, 146), but nothing is more expressive of the Turkish sensibility than the Ushak prayer rug, with its crisply outlined stepped prayer niche echoing Seljuk architecture (plate 142).

To the West of Ushak rises the hilly region surrounding Bergama. Many rugs from the surrounding area are named after this is the town out which they were sold (plate 148). Of the many types of rugs produced most are of a smaller size, less than 8 by 6 feet. The boldly geometric patterns recall Caucasian Kazak designs. Some of the finest Bergama rugs are the 'Kiz,' or wedding rugs, traditionally woven by the bride to commemorate the great event of her life. The field usually contains a hexagonal medallion and stars, with a wavy band running along the broad border. The typical colors are yellow, sand, apricot, and light blue in delicate harmonies, giving these rugs a 'peaches and cream' aura.

To the North lie the towns of Ezine and Cannakkle which weave rugs that follow in the tradition of the Holbein pattern rugs of the 16th century. These rugs typically have an orangey red color.

Along the coast to the South lies the town of Melas which has a long tradition of making prayer rugs warmly colored in reds, yellows, and aubergine with wefts that are dyed red. The prayer arch is usually pinched in by two triangular wedges near the top; this perhaps represents a geometrized version of the mihrab as depicted in Ottoman court prayer rugs. The border designs vary little over time, thus illustrating the conservative nature of this tradition. A very unusual example of this type, with its unmistakable color scheme and red wefts identifying it as a Melas is illustrated in plate 157. Another type from this region, often called Karova Melas, consists of vertical panels carrying an angular stem meander with cockscomb-like attachments and turtle medallions. Further along the Mediterranean coast is the village of Makri, now called Fethiye, which also produced brilliant prayer rugs. These and the secular weavings have a design made up of one, in many prayer rugs, or two vertical panels of differing colors, containing large geometric devices in strong yellows, blues, and reds, highlighted by a predominance of ivory.

In Central Anatolia, Konya and Ladik have long histories of rug making. Konya became the capital of the Seljuk in 1080. Many rugs from the surrounding area are called Konya but can be placed more specifically. However these rugs have certain common characteristics which include a loose weave, very lustrous wool, bold rather than intricate designs, the use of red/orange. Also many of the older rugs have rows of lappets, small arrow shaped forms, as an extra border on the ends of the rugs. One large group of Konya rugs which demonstrate why these rugs are so avidly collected, date from circa 1800, and have rich yellow grounds decorated with large Memling guls or simple large medallions repeated in the yellow ground field.

Ladik rugs have a recognizable style characterized in their prayer rugs (plate 158) that rank especially high in the pantheon of Anatolian prayer rugs, the early types include the triple-arch-and-column prayer design. Later examples from the late 18th century are known for their blazing reds and clear blues articulating an open field and the crenellations on top of the mihrab have hooks attached to each step, and curled leaf forms in the white panel above the mihrab. The horizontal panel, above

Turkish Rugs

the field in the older examples, is a unique feature of Anatolian prayer rugs and in Ladik rugs in particular.

To the North of Konya approaching Ankara are Kirshehir and Mudjur towns that have produced their share of outstanding prayer rugs with characteristic color schemes. Kirshehir favored a cochineal derived cherry-red or magenta field accented by light green, or blue. Their rugs sometimes employed as many as a dozen different colors, yet maintained a sparkling clarity of tone. A mosaic-like effect is produced by the delicately worked main borders articulated into square compartments containing angular flowers in a diamond pattern. Mudjur prayer rugs have a stepped mihrab usually with a red ground and green spandrels, and a border design of floral rosettes that is found on nearly all of these prayer rugs.

Sivas, located near the Persian border in Eastern Anatolia, borrowed many color and design schemes from Tabriz. The tight weave and rich earth tones of Tabriz appear in the Sivas rug (plates 160, 161, 162). Also influenced by Persia, Angora rugs borrowed many motifs such as the boteh for its fine rugs, woven in the famed Angora goat hair.

A few traditional Anatolian village rug types are surrounded by a sea of less easily identifiable rugs also meriting the label 'Anatolian.' In addition to the settled peasant population, a large number of nomads, frequently of Kurdish decent, roam the hills and valleys of Asia Minor and are known by the collective name of Yuruk. The shaggy, boldly conceived, and coarsely knotted Yuruk rugs with braided ends appear mostly in smaller sizes and provide insulation for the tents of these wanderers. Bright colors, chiefly magenta, green, and deep blue, ivory, and a variety of natural browns form the palette of these primitive and durable rugs (Plate 159).

Anatolia has prided itself on a long tradition of flat-weaves. The patterns favor extreme geometric designs that conform to the limitations of the technique. Kilims serve as hangings, coverlets, and prayer mats. Of the large variety produced, most are prayer kilims and long kilims, usually 12 to 14 feet long, woven in two strips and sewn together afterward. Anatolian kilims have been receiving more attention since the publication of *The Undiscovered Kilim* by Black and Loveless, and *Kilims* by Y. Petsopoulus. Their symbology is difficult to trace but can be traced back to pre-history and the mother-goddess cults that proliferated at that time. Many important collections of kilims have been made throughout the world of Anatolian kilims in the last quarter of the 20th century, which is ironic since until some years ago these objects were seen as worthless and used to wrap around the bales of carpets exported to the West. A current spate of carbon dating of a certain group of kilims has produced dates that make these kilims three to four hundred years old.

A related flat-weave type, called cicim (djidjim) is also used for curtains and coverlets. Cicim are embroidered or brocaded kilims, with the loose ends of the weft-face embroidery pattern hanging free in the back.

The Turkish and Anatolian traditions of rug weaving are as rich and diverse as that of Persia, and the two traditions are inexplicably linked, however the colors and designs of many Turkish rugs are unmistakable in the context of the world of woven art. The importance of Turkish weaving lies in the fact it has the earliest extant body of weavings currently known, the Seljuk carpets found in Konya, and that aspects of this tradition can still be seen in weavings produced today and even more clearly in the products of the 19th century. The aesthetic charm of all levels of the weaving tradition are obvious to all.

plate **136** | Ghiordes
19th century
12'4" x 17'0" (3.76 x 5.18m)
This signifies the growth in the
production of large carpets in
the second half of the 19th
century that were made for
export to Europe. This carpet
reproduces the designs used in
Ghiordes prayer and Ushak rugs
from the 17th century on a large
scale in beautifully muted colors.

plate **137** | USHAK CARPET
19th century
13′2″ x 20′11″ (4.01 x 4.88m)
*The athleticism of the lattice and
palmettes allow this carpet to
delineate large spaces that seem
to create another level of design.
The brilliance of the color and
design create a truly magnificent
carpet.*

Turkish Rugs

plate **138** | Ushak
mid 17th century
7′ x 10′ (2.13 x 3.05m)

*This important classical rug
shows the early medallion carpet
tradition of the Ottoman court.
It is unusual in its size and scale
of design. The beauty of the blue
on red tracery and the manner
in which the design is
punctuated by details in
different colors demonstrates the
skill of the 17th century
designers.*

plate **140** | Ushak Carpet
19th century
11′4″ x 11′9″ (3.45 x 3.58m)
*Blocks of design are repeated
throughout the field. The space
between these repeating
elements is created by
imaginative design and a strong
ground color.*

plate **141** | Ushak Carpet
19th century
20′ x 28′ (6.10 x 8.53m)
*The lattice design is elongated
along the vertical axis, but is
broken by the intersection of the
lattice by small white flowers
and leaves, thereby creating a
variety of different perspectives
to the composition.*

Turkish Rugs

plate **142** | Ushak Rug
20th century.
3'7" x 5'8" (1.09 x 1.73m)
This rug is interesting since it's design is copied from a famous 16th century Ushak rug now in the Islamic Art Museum in Berlin, Germany. This rug belonged to, and was published, by the famous rug collector Willem Von Bode. When the rug reappeared after having been in a private collection for 33 years, its border had been cut off. It was subsequently published in this form, and it is from this later version that the copies, such as this rug were made with only two minor borders. This rug is an important historical document of design evolution.

plate **143** | Ushak
Late 19th century
11' x 13'3" (3.35 x 4.04m)
*Ushak that displays Western
influence of soft colors and
sparsely design rugs of
this period. This type of rugs is
still in great demand, especially
in the United States and Europe.*

Turkish Rugs

plate **144** | Ushak
13'7" x 19'4" (4.14 x 5.89m)
A very attractive honey and melon colored rug, where compartmental design is interconnected with the free flowing river, makes this a very unique design.

Turkish Rugs

plate **145** | Ushak Carpet
19th century
12'3" x 13'9" (3.73 x 4.19m)
*The medallion design of this
carpet is derived from the
Smyrna carpets that were
exported to Europe from
modern-day Izmir from the 16th
century onwards. The design has
become more geometric since its
original inception, however the
complexity of the inter-
relationship between the
elements has remained the same.*

plate **146** | Ushak
7′8″ x 9′3″ (2.34 x 2.82m)
*Another interesting color
combination for an Ushak of the
early 20th century.*

Turkish Rugs

plate **147** | Ushak Carpet
Late 19th century
12′6″ x 13′ (3.81 x 3.96m)

*This carpet epitomizes a certain
Ushak carpet of the late 19th
century. They were produced in
relatively large numbers, and
usually have wool foundation
dyed the same color as the field.
They are basely woven with
vivid colors and open large-scale
design.*

plate **148** | BERGAMA CARPET
20th century
11'6" x 15' (3.51 x 4.57m)
A classic design in cheerful colors. The original field design is of particular note.

Turkish Rugs

plate **149** | Ushak
4′ x 6′5″ (1.22 x 1.96m)
A reduction of design originally made for much larger rugs of the 20th century, the artist has creatively reinterpreted the scale and design to fit so beautifully in such a small frame. The yellow and green colors in the border on a red field give this rug a great balance.

plate **150** | MELAS
19th century
3'2" x 4'5" (0.97 x 1.35m)
*This prayer rug has classic
columns associated with West
Anatolian prayer rugs from the
17th century. The feathered
leaves, bright colors and stylized
tree of life are typical of these
rugs.*

    TURKISH RUGS

plate **151** | GHIORDES PRAYER
4'3" x 5'10" (1.30 x 1.78m)
*This early 19th century Ghiordes
with classical prayer design and
the cool steel coloring has a
special appeal and an impressive
elegance.*

plate **152** | Kayseri Carpet
20th century
9'6" x 13' (2.90 x 3.96m)
Rugs have been made in the city of Kayseri in central Anatolia for centuries and many have mercerized cotton in their foundations and pile. This carpet has an interesting design that incorporates Persian and Turkish classical carpet design including that of a 17th Ladik prayer rug. The mixture of a central medallion and complete rug designs that are used as individual elements is not commonly seen in these carpets.

plate **153** | GHIORDES PRAYER RUG
Late 19th century
3'10" x 5'2" (1.17 x 1.57m).
*This prayer rug is typical of its
design type, made in Ghiordes,
West Anatolia, but this piece is
unusual due to its particularly
light coloring. The rectangular
panels containing cloudbands
above and below the field are
related to those that appear in
17th century examples made for
the Ottoman court.*

plate **154** | GHIORDES PRAYER
4'4" x 5'8" (1.32 x 1.73m)
This wonderful rug is made in the middle of 19th century with distinctive colors usually associated with rugs from Melas. The plain ground of dark blue prayer niche surrounded by the inner and outer borders have the same pistachio green and soft blue. The upper flowerbeds give extra dimensions, connecting tulip flowers around the prayer niche.

Turkish Rugs

plate **155** | Hereke Carpet
20th century
13′ x 15′3″ (3.96 x 4.65m)
The design of this carpet shows
the European influence that
many of the large carpets from
these workshops had.

plate **156** | Silk Hereke
3′5″ x 5′ (1.04 x 1.52m)
*Typical of 20th century silk
Hereke rugs that are continuing
the same designs of centuries
ago with a new color pallet.*

Turkish Rugs

plate **157** | Melas Rug
19th century
3'9" x 5'6" (1.14 x 1.68m)
The rug has a Baroque design
which was popular in the mid
19th century. Although this
town is normally associated with
prayer rugs it should be noted
that this design does incorporate
two prayer arches at each end of
the field. This type of double-
ended design is an important
part of the Turkish rug
repertoire, and is found in rugs
from the 16th century.

plate **158** | LADIK
17th century
3'10" x 5'9" (1.17 x 1.75m)
This classic Ladik prayer rug design is influenced by Laleh dervi period where intermingling of French and Turkish artists resulted in new ways of interpreting floral patterns.

Turkish Rugs

plate **160** | Sivas
Circa 1900
12′ x 16′6″ (3.66 x 5.03m)
*A decorative Sivas with soft
colors of Western liking.*

Turkish Rugs

plate **161** | Sivas Carpet
Circa 1900
10′ x 12′8″ (3.05 x 3.86m)
The beautifully subtle colors of this carpet illustrate the skill of this carpet weaving center's designers.

plate **162** | Sᴠᴀꜱ Cᴀʀᴘᴇᴛ
Circa 1900
11′5″ x 14′1″ (3.48 x 4.29m)
The weavers from this area
copied designs from other
weaving centers. This design is
associated with Tabriz rugs from
Northwest Persia.

Turkish Rugs

Caucasian Rugs

The Caucasus is a complex mosaic of different races, religions and languages. The area has long served as a haven for refugees driven from their homelands and as a corridor for migrations. For thousands of years it was used as a passage between Asia and Europe, and during this time it was invaded and occupied by many different peoples.

The region's long and complex history has brought about an incredible ethnic diversity that can be difficult to unravel. A distinction that is often made is one of language, with true Caucasians – those who speak languages not found outside the region – on the one hand, and those of Indo-European or Turkic stock on the other. Muslims, Christians and Jews can all be found in the area: Armenians and Georgians are Christians, while Turkic groups and Kurds are Muslims. In addition, a large population of Jews lived in this area until the 1990s, when many migrated to Israel, after the Republics of Armenia, Georgia and Azerbaijan established their own rule following the downfall of the Soviet Union. Geographically, true Caucasians are divided into groups from the Northwest, the Northeast and the South.

The Transcaucasian region is bordered by Iran, Turkey, and Russia, and takes its name from a rugged mountain range which stretches 700 miles from the mouth of the Kuban River on the Black Sea to the Apsheron peninsula on the Caspian Sea. At their peak, the Caucas mountains reach 17,000 feet. Across the Kura River valley to the South, the lesser Caucasus slope more gently, and grassy hills provide ample pasture for sheep. In this breathtaking mountain setting, one of the most sophisticated rug-producing cultures ever known came into being.

The fiercely independent nomads of the regions repelled enemies for centuries in order to maintain control of their land. Their rugs reflect this bold, martial spirit and are valued for their robust geometric patterns as well as for their well-balanced designs in vividly contrasting colors (Plate 166).

Although Caucasians have been active weavers for millennia, the earliest surviving pile-woven carpets from the area, so-called 'Dragon Carpets', date only from the 17th century. Fine examples from this era – clearly a golden age for weaving in the region – are housed in museums all over the world and are widely published. The majority of fine Caucasian rugs available on the market today belong to the 19th and early 20th centuries.

In the early 19th century, the Russians took over Daghestan, Georgia, Armenia, and Azerbaijan – the heartlands of Caucasian weaving. Yet were it not for Russian intervention in the area, it is possible that Caucasian rugs would never have reached Europe in such quantities or have enjoyed such widespread popularity. Inevitably, this European

demand affected productivity and designs, and many regions, most notably Karabagh and Zeikhur, began to produce weavings with floral motifs in conscious imitation of the Savonneries, Aubussons and Axminsters of Western Europe (Plates 178, 179, 181).

In the 1930s, production was shifted to state-run factories and collectives, but these more recent rugs lack the inspiration of the traditional pieces. The situation was further complicated by the arrival of copies on the market, made by Russian and Pakistani artisans. Without the unique wool of Caucasian mountain sheep and the high quality dyeing of the area, these weavings can not compare with the originals.

A final blow to the Caucasian rug-making cultures came at the end of World War II. The obstinately autonomous peoples of the Caucasus never accepted the doctrines of Communism, and many fled during the war throughout Europe or volunteered to serve under the German Reich. At the end of the War, under the promise of Allied protection, some returned to the Caucasus, only to be massacred by the Soviets. Stalin deported many of the remaining tribes to Siberia. Such upheavals, the consequence of which can still be seen in the politics of the region today, undoubtedly played a major part in the demise of rug weaving in the Caucasus.

Unlike many modern Russian Caucasian rugs with cotton warp and weft, the traditional rugs of the Caucasus were almost always knotted on a wool warp and weft. The lean mountain sheep of the cold highlands provided lustrous fleece that looks and feels like silk. Today this glossy wool is one of the identifying characteristics of Caucasian rugs. The wool is usually left naturally brown or white for the warp, while the weft is often dyed pink or red, particularly in Kazaks. The top and bottom ends of the rugs frequently exhibit fringes braided into plaits (plate 171). The sides are wrapped with white wool or cotton in Shirvans, blue wool in Kubas, and red or multi-colored wool in other types, particularly Genjes (plates 164, 185).

The wool from the lower Caucasus, although still of excellent quality, does not match the high-altitude wool for warmth or softness and density of pile when woven. So, in the lowland regions of Kuba, Shirvan, and Baku, weavers seem to favor a shorter pile, while in the mountainous areas of Kazak and Gendje, for example, a longer, shaggier and warmer structure is favored, comparable to the so-called *yatak* or bed rugs of Anatolia.

Caucasian rugs were traditionally dyed with natural dyes of the best quality, until the introduction of synthetic dyes in the second half of the 19th century. Used in lively juxtapositions, these bright colors perfectly complement and enhance their forceful geometric designs. On the coarser weavings of the Caucasus these designs are usually conceived on a bold scale, as on Kazak rugs, where angular medallions and large abstract shapes dominate the field (plates 166, 172, 174). By contrast, the finer, lowland weavings favor tighter designs that are finely executed. All Caucasian rugs tend to be framed by multiple rows of borders.

Often Caucasian rugs contain simplified, rectilinear renditions of familiar Persian motifs, such as the *boteh*. Rows of geometric floral ele-

plate **164** | GENJE RUG
Southwest Caucasus
19th century
3′5″ x 8′3″ (1.04 x 2.51m)
*This rug has the medallions of
rugs associated with the village
of Schulaver in the Kazak
region, but the hooked diamond
motif with a bird center in the
border is common to Akstafa
rugs.*
*This rug's rich colors and
lustrous wool are typical of the
Caucasian rug.*

plate **163**
FACHRALO KAZAK PRAYER RUG
Southwest Caucasus
Dated 1339AH/AD 1920
3′9″ x 5′9″ (1.14 x 1.75m)
*This prayer rug is a later
member of a rare group of
prayer rugs, the earliest date
from the early 19th century and
contain silk in their construction.
They all have this large central
medallion beneath the mihrab
and many are dated. The
treatment of the prayer arch and
the lozenge devices in the field
are common to all the rugs in
this group.*

ments in diagonally alternating colors and/or within stripes of contrasting colors appear frequently, as in the Gendje illustrated in plate 164. Many rugs feature reciprocal patterns; so at times the ground color itself can assume the elements of a design, creating a sophisticated optical game (plate 184).

Caucasian weavers incorporated many familiar features from their daily lives into their designs, punctuating the larger abstract forms with tiny human figures; domestic animals including dogs, birds, and camels (plates 173, 174); or flowers. The educated eye can also pick out boats, houses, graves, and combs. The precise significance of these motifs to the weaver is debatable, but clearly a kind of symbolism may be traced back to the region's ancestral tribal beliefs. Christian Caucasians commonly used cruciform motifs, such as the eight-pointed Maltese cross, and even depicted churches on some rugs; while Muslims favored more abstract designs, particularly on prayer rugs, perhaps as a result of the restriction on representation of animate objects in Islam. Nevertheless, Caucasian rugs from traditionally Islamic tribes often feature shepherds, riders on horseback, and weavers.

Certain symbols, such as the swastika, are held to be signs of good luck or provide protection against the evil eye. However, as these designs were passed on from generation to generation, it seems likely that their original significance became forgotten, and that many either acquired a secondary meaning or simply became decorative. Caucasian rugs belong to a vibrant folk culture, and as such they reflect not only the life of village communities but also in many cases the personality of the weaver. Weaving was usually carried out in the home or even tent by women who rarely, if ever, used designs mapped out on cartoons. They would work from memory and during the creation of a rug enjoyed improvising on traditional designs to instill something of themselves into their weaving.

Caucasian rugs were woven on simple, upright looms that were relatively small. As a result most weavings from the region are usually 3 to 5 feet wide and 3 to 7 feet long (with the exception of runners, which can reach 20 feet). The loom size was perfectly sufficient for one of the most important objects in Islamic ritual, the prayer rug, which measures roughly 3 by 5 feet. These rugs often contain small amulets, latch-hook diamonds to avert the evil eye, or combs to symbolize cleanliness. Frequently, the weaver would also include dates woven into the rug's design (plates 163, 183).

Two main geographic units of Caucasian rugs can be made, and we will discuss them in reference to these: those from Central and Southern areas, typified by Kazak, Karabagh, Gendje, Talish, Moghan and Lenkoran; and those from the Northeast; typified by the Shirvan and Kuba. Attribution to these areas is largely based on design, color and structure, but with the Caucasus it is important to remember that precise ethnic or geographic pinpointing is often a matter of intelligent guesswork.

Central and Southern Caucasus

The Kazak district was one of the most prolific rug-making areas of the last century. Stretching from Tiflis in Georgia to the more arid plains of Erivan in Armenia, and from Kars to the Moghan steppes, this region has been home to a huge diversity of races and peoples. Christian Armenians, Muslim Kossacks, Kurds, and Turko-Tartars formed the principal weaving communities. Convention divides Kazak rugs alone into at least eleven different categories, and there is considerable dispute among experts about the validity of such classification. The more commonly employed and collected of these types are the so-called Sewan, Karachov, Borjalou, Lori Pambak and the very rare tree designs Kazaks (plates 170, 171, 173).

Sewan Kazak rugs take their name from Lake Sewan, the area around which they are thought to have been produced. They bear an elongated Maltese cross framing the central design, which in many ways resembles a shield, hence the name 'Shield Kazak' occasionally used in the trade. This heraldic emblem, outlined in white, may hark back to ancient Turkmen double-arrowhead motifs, but the source for the design is almost certainly pre-Islamic. Some versions of the Sewan Kazak with more rounded shields are thought to represent water basins in a land where water is scarce. In this example, the unusual border features curled tendrils separated by stepped triangles.

Closely related to the Sewan is the much sought-after type from the Karachov area. These design centers on a large octagon, perhaps related to the Turkmen gül, surrounded by projecting hooks which recall ram's horns. These 'latch-hooks' are found in many Caucasian rugs are occasionally interpreted as symbols of happiness. Similar hooked devices can be seen in the corners of the field, along with small rectangular boxes. The main border frames the composition with variants of a popular pattern called the 'serrated leaf and chalice', although the chalice may in fact be a floral device. Many collectors particularly value a deep emerald green as the most desirable field color, especially if this is combined with a yellow ground border.

To the North of the Karachov district, vibrantly primal rugs, known as Borjalou, were produced (plates 166, 170). Concentric diamond lozenges are with hooked outlines are placed on a bright tomato-red field, while a scattering of smaller ornaments suggestive of flowers, cradles, jugs, mirrors, and other symbolic objects frequently serve to break up this powerful design. The wide border carries a reciprocal arrangement of the same hooked medallions halved into triangular shapes. Borjalous were often made in relatively large sizes. Kurd Kazaks are distinctive with Persian influences.

While the Southern and Central areas of the Caucasus are actually home to a diverse array of weaving traditions, a number of these types, especially those woven in and around the town of Gendje and in the Karabagh region, are sometimes mistakenly referred to as Kazaks on account of certain superficial similarities. Other traditions, most notably those of the Talish district far in the South, have a more distinctive quality.

224

Gendje rugs, from the town known today as Kirovabad in Azerbaijan, bear a close resemblance to Kazaks, but are lighter in color, and have a preponderance of white and light blue. The edges are finished with multi-color overcasting rather than the traditional browns and reds. Instead of major medallions, Gendje weavers preferred small repeated geometric figures with diagonal color arrangements (plate 164).

The so-called 'Eagle' or 'Sunburst Kazak' is said to come from the village of Chelaberd in Karabagh, over 100 miles South of the area where the main body of Kazaks are made. The flamboyant 'spoked' medallions peculiar to this group may derive from the elements found in the earlier 'Dragon Carpets'. Other scholars interpret these bird-form medallions as versions of the 19th-century Russian Imperial eagle, while others still regard the medallion as a floral in origin. Whatever the significance, the borders cut through the design so as to suggest continuous and infinite space, with the continuation of the design implicit beyond the borders. The 'Eagle Kazak' almost always has an ivory border with linked stars and a saw-tooth secondary border.

From Chondzoresk, another well-known Karabagh design is often referred to as the 'Cloudband Kazak', after the four angular shapes arranged within two or more bold medallions. The cloudband motif is believed to be Far Eastern in origin and perhaps denotes the celestial realm.

An earlier style of rug made in Karabagh relates closely to certain Northwest Persian designs (plate 182). This outstanding early 19th-century Karabagh is clearly based on the Persianate Herati pattern (plate 168). The rich floral latticework, intricately curvilinear in Persia, appears here in an angular and simplified form. The deep saffron yellow found on this piece rarely occurs in later examples and gives a strong indication of age. The red and white reciprocal minor borders add an unmistakably Caucasian touch to an otherwise Persian design. A deep reddish purple appears in many rugs from this same period. Russian rule of this area eventually brought with it the adoption of European designs, and a predilection for realistically drawn floral elements (plates 178, 179).

To the Southeast of the Karabagh district lie the Talish villages, where a striking form of long rug was woven (Plate 184). The central field most commonly consists of a single deep blue strip, sometimes punctuated by a few small rosettes. A rich white border usually carries large rounded rosettes alternating with four small angular flowerheads. Talishes feel velvety and their workmanship is finer than most Karabaghs or Kazaks. These particularly elegant Caucasian rugs have become quite rare.

Lenkoran ranks as one of the chief towns of the Talish district. A very distinctive and highly prized type of runner was woven here. Measuring approximately 10' by 4', these rugs feature crab-like medallions and small octagons, depicted on a deep blue ground (plate 183). These motifs draw upon the Mongol tradition of the Tartar tribes who lived in the Southern Caucasus from the 14th century onward. One of the most remarkable features of Lenkoran rugs is their thick, velvety wool, which is usually clipped to a medium length.

Travelling to the extreme Southeast, we reach the region of Moghan, where the arid rocky steppe provided the last refuge for the nomadic way of life. The weavers of Moghan wove rugs mostly in runner sizes and favored light pastel shades. They employed geometric floral and leaf devices in their designs, similar to those found on many Kazaks and Talishes. Rows of octagonal patterns surrounded by hooked crosses were also typical, as were polygons, executed with extreme precision in soft, lustrous wool. Few Moghans appear on the market today, and those that do frequently fall short of the high standards for which these weavers are renowned (plate 186).

The North and Northeast Caucasus

A major group of Caucasian rugs comes from the Kuba-Shirvan region along the Eastern Shore of the Caspian Sea. Often Kuba rugs are very difficult to distinguish from Shirvan rugs, but, in general, both types exhibit a finer weave and shorter pile than found on Kazaks. Designs tend to be less bold and more intricate, although large-scale patterns resembling Kazaks do occur. Many designs take their name from the village that originally produced them, but by the 19th century, these designs were widely copied, making identification by pattern alone unreliable. Often the only clues to origin are small structural details, such as the finish of the sides and ends, or the degree of depression in the warps, observable on the back of the rug. In this section we will discuss Shirvans, including Baku, Chila, Marasali, and Surahani, Kubas, Perepedil, Chichi, and Zeikhur, Daghestans, and Derbents.

In general, Shirvan rugs may be distinguished by darker warp threads, white wool or cotton selvedges, and smooth backs with the warps all lying on the same level. The three-medallion design occurs frequently (plates 165, 189). Prayer rugs were a favorite, with the most popular coming from Marasali, known for its rugs with multicolor angular botehs on a midnight blue ground framed by a border of bird shapes. These birds have been variously identified as parrots, symbols of good luck or of deliverance from misfortune, following the legend that Genghis Khan was saved by his pet parrot.

The city of Baku, today a thriving oil center in Azerbaijan, was known for its rugs as far back as the 18th century. In contrast to the robust texture of Kazaks, Baku rugs feel thin and pliable. While Kazaks display vigorous colors, Bakus rely on subtle effects in a limited range of earth tones and turquoises. These rugs are also notable for their intricate border designs with variants of Kufic (early Islamic) script and a complex play of interlocking lozenges.

From Khila, a village in the Baku district, come some of the finest early examples of Caucasian weaving, characterised by subtle designs in rich pistachios, ambers and lavenders with polychrome striped borders. The weavers of Khila adapted a bold, almost three-dimensional design of cruciform shapes and güls, reminiscent of Shirvans. Rugs with this design have a particularly a rough feel to their back. Like Marasali prayer rugs, many Khila rugs also depict rows of highly geometric botehs against deep marine blue ground.

Related to the earlier Khilas, Surahani rugs have a similar subdued chromatic range. These relatively rare rugs favor striking combinations of glowing earth tones set against pale fields.

plate **165** | Shirvan Rug
East Caucasus
19th century
3′6″ x 4′8″ (1.07 x 1.42m)
Many Shirvan area rugs have designs influenced by those of other rug weaving regions. The medallions here are usually seen on the Sumakh carpets made in the Kuba area. However they are excellently converted into the pile format by the clever Shirvan weaver.

Caucasian Rugs

Immediately to the North of Shirvan lies the great rug-export center of Kuba. Rugs such as the one illustrated in plate 187 would be difficult to distinguish from Marasali weaving purely in terms of design. The structure of Kubas is often the best indicator of origin. On the back, these rugs tend to be less smooth than Shirvans because alternate warps lie depressed. Kubas were especially famous for their beautiful blues; and even their selvedges employed blue wool. Also of note are Kuba rugs with columns of highly distinctive 'Lesghi' stars. These wonderful motifs take their name from the Lesghians to the North, who were once thought to have woven rugs with such designs. 'Lesghi' stars are variants of the Maltese cross and are thought to refer to a divine celestial presence.

Another medallion rug woven in the same silky pile and fine weave found in most Kubas originates from the neighborhood of Zeikhur. On this type, the medallions consist of elaborate cross-like motifs, which are often transformed into highly stylized dragons or flowers. Another variety of Zeikhur rug, however, adopted a European-style 'cabbage-rose' motif, rendered in crimson and pink in a forceful Caucasian manner. The 'Running Dog' border commonly frames these rugs. The field pattern of another Zeikhur derives from the so-called 'Bijov' design, named after a village in the Shirvan area.

South of Shirvan, close to the Caspian Sea, the weavers of Perepedil wove some of the most distinctive rugs of the Caucasus. Easily recognizable by their repeat designs of ram horns, known as *wurma*, etched in white against a deep blue indigo field complemented by borders and minor designs in earth tones. Frequently the border bears a star design or a vase and chalice motif, and on occasion a Kufic pattern of the kind found on Baku rugs.

Chichi rugs may easily be identified by their wide borders with alternating quatrefoil rosette and diagonal band motif. Made in a village to the Southwest of Perepedil in the Kuba district, these finely woven, low-pile rugs usually feature a field of compact stepped polygons. They are highly sought after by Caucasian rug connoisseurs.

Along the extreme Northern edge of the Caucasus runs Daghestan, 'The Land of the Mountains', whose capital is Derbent. This region, most celebrated for its precisely woven prayer rugs, continues to produce a large quantity of rugs of various types. The Lesghian tribes of these mountains made tightly woven rugs with a firm, compact feel. Exquisite white ground prayer rugs with honeycomb lattice flower-head patterns are excellent examples of the fine workmanship of Daghestan.

Flatweave

Caucasian rug districts produced various flatweaves that go by the names of *palas, kilim, sumakh, verneh,* and *sileh*. These were intended mostly for home use as hangings, coverlets, carriage covers, and bags. *Verneh* and *sileh* are highly individual types of flatweave that may be examples of an indigenous Caucasian tradition. The former usually feature red, blue, and green rectangular compartments containing fanciful animals, while the latter are well-known for their angular 'S'-shaped dragons covered with a multitude of small scales; woven in two panels, meant to be attached (plate 190).

The Caucasus has a particularly rich tradition of kilim production. Examples include large (up to 10 by 6 feet) pieces woven in the slit-weave technique (plates 191, 192, 193). Designs range from simple banded stripes to repeats of more complex hooked 'X'-shapes or polygons in red, white, blue, and green. Avar Area known for fine Kilims in rare occasions produced extraordinary pile rugs.

If the word *sumakh* is any indication of the origin of this technique, it may well have evolved in the Caucasus in the town of Shemaka. *Sumakhs* were made all along the Caspian in a variety of patterns including medallions and overall repeats.

plate **166** | Borjalu Kazak Rug
Southwest Caucasus
19th century
4′ x 7′7″ (1.32 x 2.31m)
*This beautiful triple medallion
rug has borders that are usually
found on rugs from Daghestan.
The multi-layered diamond
medallions on the edge of the
field are quite arresting.*

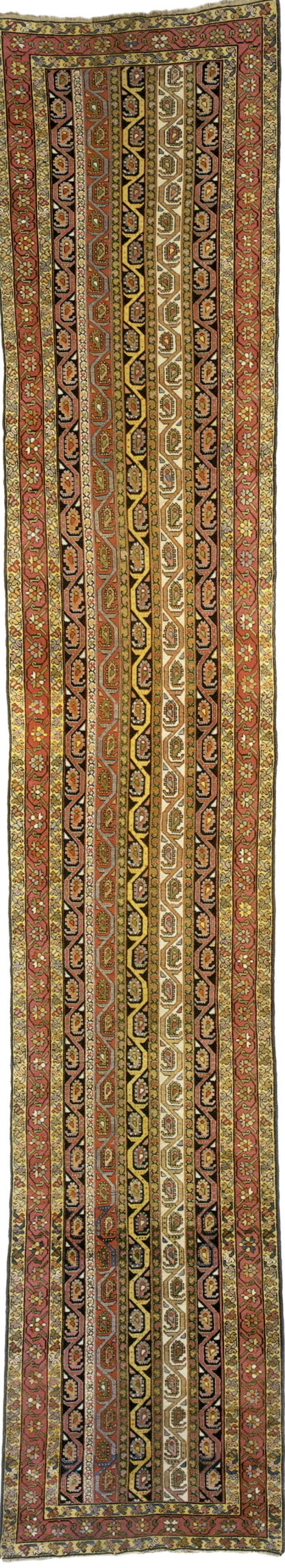

plate **167** | KARABAGH RUNNER
West Caucasus
Late 19th century
3′6″ x 19′6″ (1.07 x 5.94m)
*The palette used in this
exceptionally vivid and colorful
runner is characteristic of a
group of Karabagh weavings
made at the turn of the century:
yellow, green and crimson pink
obtained by the use of cochineal.
The field design of stripes of
meandering vines curling
around chunky botehs is
sometimes used as borders.
(one of a pair)*

plate **168** | KARABAGH RUG
South Caucasus
Late 19th century
4′ x 9′5″ (1.07 x 5.94m)
*The two tones of pink used are
particularly attractive and give
the roses a realistic texture. The
very large scale Herati ground
typifies the versatility of the
Karabagh weavers at adapting
Persian designs.*

Caucasian Rugs

plate **169** | Karabagh Rug
Southwest Caucasus
19th century
4′7″ x 7′7″ (1.40 x 2.31m)

The brilliant graphic design of radiating hooked polygons has a power and majesty that is obvious and striking. Although this design is one used in Borjalu Kazaks, the borders are pure Karabagh. The salt and pepper warps, called this as they have speckled effect from the intertwining of black and white threads to make the warp, are those of Karabagh and this is the most appropriate attribution.

plate **170** | Borjalu Kazak Rug
Southwest Caucasus
19th century
6'3" x 8'4" (1.91 x 2.54m)
*The aggressive hooked
medallions in the main border of
this carpet and the dizzying
elements inside these are
extraordinarily graphic. The
roundels in the yellow minor
border are found on older Kazak
rugs.*

Caucasian Rugs

plate **171**
Lori Pambak Kazak Rug
Southwest Caucasus
19th century
5′ x 7′6″ (1.52 x 2.29m)
*The combination of designs
inside these medallions are
characteristic of rugs from the
Lori Pambak village. The
beautiful wine glass and leaf
border is very popular in Kazak
rugs.*

plate **172** | Kazak Rug
Southwest Caucasus
19th century
5′8″ x 7′7″ (1.73 x 2.31m)
These star medallions and
rosettes are common to two
different types of Kazak, the
most famous of which are the
eponymous Star Kazaks. The
abrashed red ground gives a
depth to the overall composition,
creating the appearance that the
motifs hover over the ground.

Caucasian Rugs

plate **173** | Tree Kazak Rug
Southwest Caucasus
19th century
5'6" x 6'10" (1.68 x 2.08m)
These rugs are loved by
collectors of the bold Caucasian
rugs. The trees are inspired by
those that are found on the
great Safavid carpets. The
medallions on this group of
carpets are always similar to
those on this rug but the smaller
medallions are less common. The
abundance of animals and
people in the field are of great
charm and add to the vitality of
the rug.

plate **174** | Karabagh Carpet
Southwest Caucasus
Dated 1899
4'7" x 8'9" (1.40 x 2.97m)
This is an interpretation of a Kazak design and is full of Armenian elements, notably the date written in the Christian tradition. The profusion of people and wider and less aggressively hooked medallions shows the influence of the Karabagh weaver. Compare this rug with that of the Kazak, plate 183, to see the different treatment of a similar theme.

Caucasian Rugs

plate **175** | KAZAK RUG

Southwest Caucasus
20th century
5'10" x 7'10" (1.78 x 2.39)
*This rug shows signs of Persian
influence but the structure and
colors of a Caucasian weaving.
The layout of the medallion
design and the numerous filler
elements in the spandrels show
that this carpet was made in a
weaving community that had
access to the designs of the
weaving districts in Azerbaijan
just over the border.*

plate **176** | Genje Rug
Southwest Caucasus
19th century
3′6″ x 9′ (1.07 x 2.74m)
*The best Genje rugs derive great
strength from their simple
designs, as is evident here.*

plate **177** | Kazak Rug
Southwest Caucasus
19th century
3'10" x 7'4" (1.17 x 2.24m)
*A interesting rug since it has the
hooked medallions usually
associated with Borjalu village
rugs and a border typical to rugs
from much further East, near
the Caspian Sea. The use of
areas of white creates an added
dimension to the design.*

plate **178** and plate **179**
KARABAGH RUGS
South Caucasus
Circa 1900
Both 3'9" x 8' (1.12 x 2.64m)
This pair formed from one larger
rug, has European designs of
floral bouquets popular with the
weavers of the Karabagh region,
many of whom were Armenian.

Caucasian Rugs

*The carpet has an interpretation
of European flowers that the
Armenian weavers of Karabagh
favored in the late 19th century.
Interestingly the design lays
these flowers out in a manner
similar to the Kuba shield
carpets of the 17th and 18th
centuries. The design is given
added vitality by the white
outlining of the flowers against
a midnight-blue background.
The addition of this small
detailing creates a completely
effect.*

242

plate **181** | Karabagh Runner
Southwest Caucasus
20th century
3′9″ x 6′ (1.14 x 1.83m)
This carpet exhibits the scrolling vines and roses in a European manner. These carpets are much sought after by the decorative market.

Caucasian Rugs

plate **182** | KARABAGH RUNNER
Southwest Caucasus
19th century
3'3" x 18'5" (0.99 x 5.61m)
The deep indigo ground is elegantly framed by small white spandrels, while the perfectly executed border system is typical of Baku Khila carpets of the early 19th century.

plate **183** | LENKORAN
19th century
3'6" x 12'5" (1.07 x 3.78m)
This runner is from the middle period of the 19th century just at the time that the weaving revival was starting. The exceptional clarity of colors, the exuberance of the hooked designs radiating from the medallions indicate that this is a rare early piece and consequently highly valued. The date on this runner corresponds to 1860 on the Roman Calendar.

244

plate **184** | TALISH RUG
Southeast Caucasus
19th century
3'8" x 9'5" (1.12 x 2.87m)
*This exceptional rug is an
unusual variant of the normal
Talish design. Many of the rugs
woven in this region have a field
of plain blue or sometimes
green; this rug has one of the
two variation from this which
has a field filled with an all-over
design of flowerheads, the other
variation uses stars. The manner
in which the different colored
flowerheads are placed in the
ground creates a secondary
design in the rug. The border is a
rare variant of the typical
rosette border. The steel grayish
blue color is found in all the
Talish rugs and is one of the
features that makes these finely
made rugs such a desirable
and collectable weaving.
Additionally, the inscribed
Roman date, 1888 seems to
indicate that this was probably
made by American weavers.*

Caucasian Rugs

plate **185** | Genje Rug
Southwest Caucasus
19th century
3'3" x 8'7" (0.99 x 2.62m)
This carpet has the all wool foundation, multi-colored wrapping over the side cords that are typical of Genjes. Note the abrash in the medallion, part of which is red and part beige. It is thought that this is a very stylized interpretation of the garden design which is seen on many Safavid and later Persian carpets.

plate **186** | Kazak Rug
Southwest Caucasus
19th century
4'10" x 7' (1.32 x 2.13m)
A beautiful multi-medallion
Moghan design which has the
clarity of design and color that
Kazak rugs are famous for. Note
the kink in the inner borders
where the weave was
interrupted.

Caucasian Rugs

plate **188** | Shirvan Rug
East Caucasus
19th century
4' x 5' (1.20 x 1.52m)

*Pictorial rugs are rare in the
corpus of Caucasian rugs. This
depicts historic scenes that have
become highly stylized. The
background of the pictorial
panels is both unusual and
visually arresting.*

Caucasian Rugs

plate **189** | SHIRVAN RUG
East Caucasus
19th century
4'4" x 6'9" (1.32 x 2.06m)
*These rugs triple medallion are
found throughout the Caucasus.
The flaming edges to the
medallions are typical of the
Zeikur area in the Northeast
Caucasus.*

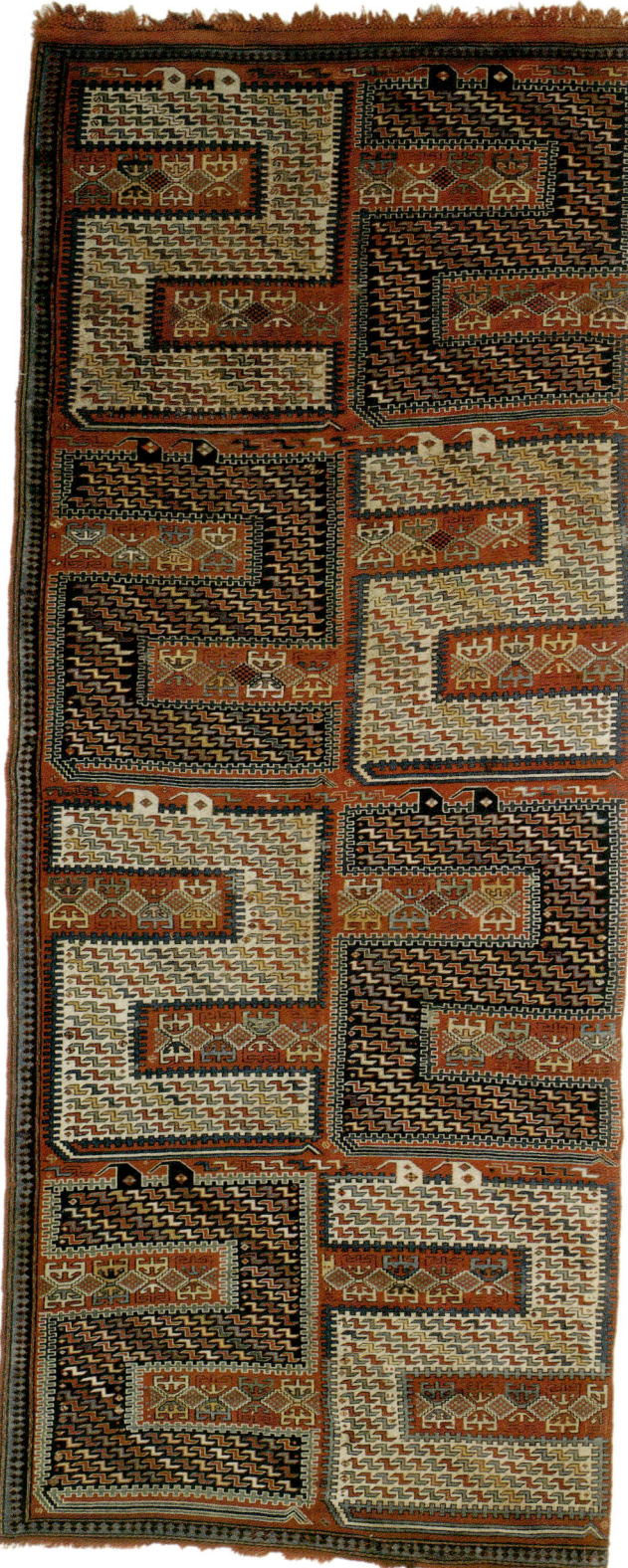

plate **190** | Sileh Rug
Northeast Causasus
19th century
7'3" x 9' (2.21 x 2.74m)
The stylized s-motifs in the flatwoven carpets referred to as being dragons – the two attachments on their heads are the horns and the tail tapers off underneath the highly impressionistic body. These covers are generally very finely woven with the pattern being part of the woven structure and not as is sometimes thought embroidered. This carpet is of exceptional beauty and age, and is a very desirable item for the collector of Caucasian weavings.

Caucasian Rugs

plate **191** | Shahsavan Kilim
South Caucasus
19th century
4'8" x 10'8" (1.42 x 3.25m)
*This simplicity of this kilim
exemplifies the attraction of
these weavings for many
collectors. The interplay between
the bands of color and the
simple geometric design creates
an interesting juxtaposition of
form and color. Areas of extra-
weft wrapping show in the areas
between the color bands are
common in the graphically
composed kilims.*

plate **192** | Sʜɪʀᴠᴀɴ Kɪʟɪᴍ
East Caucasus
19th century
5′3″ x 8′8″ (1.6 x 2.64m)
*The design of this kilim, which
would have served as a cover
within the home or even in a
tent or on a cart, shows the
strength of the Caucasian
weaver in using simple
geometric shapes and colors to
create a stunning and
contemporary juxtaposition of
color and shape. The design uses
the ideas of positive and
negative space to ha high degree
and exemplifies why these
simple weavings have gained
great popularity with many
people that collect contemporary
and graphic art.*

Caucasian Rugs

plate **193** | Kuba Kilim
Northeast Caucasus
19th century
6'6" x 10'8" (1.98 x 3.25m)
*These kilims are finely made and
would have served as covers for
various purposes, a function that
people still use them for in
contemporary interior design.*

*The carpet is a version of the
most popular design found in
sumakh rugs which have three
elongated medallions
surrounded by yellow ground
polygons. The fine weave and
sumakh technique create a
geometric design that has a
vivacity and power unexpressed
in other weavings.*

Caucasian Rugs

Turkmen Rugs

T he rugs of the Central Asian Turkmen form perhaps one of the most easily identifiable groups of weavings. Distinguished and much admired, these rugs have predominately red tones and simple geometric compositions filled with octagonal and diamond-shaped tribal insignia known as guls. The familiar repeated motifs of these rugs and trappings reflect the great age of this nomadic tradition, which may have created the oldest surviving rug, the Pazyryk Carpet.

Yet the curious paradox about these rugs is that while they would seem to be simple and easily to understand, they pose perhaps the greatest difficulties in terms of attribution, interpretation, and understanding.

The land of the Turkmen, Turkestan is a rugged terrain of arid steppe and desert, occasionally interrupted by oasis towns. The region stretches eight hundred miles East of the Caspian Sea to the Hindu Kush and Pamir Mountains, and spans four hundred miles from the Aral Sea in the North to the Kopet Dagh Mountains of Iran in the South. The few cities of Turkestan – Khiva, Merv, Bokhara, Samarkand – are built strategically around oases and serve as market centers for the region.

Although several cities have given their name to particular styles of Central Asian rugs, few were actually woven in these places, which of course adds to the confusion with attribution. Furthermore, cities are inaccurate guides to tribal attribution, as they frequently changed hands during the tumultuous 19th century. With the Tekke invasion of the Saryk and Salor territories during the last quarter of the 19th century, for example, there was a complete redistribution of tribal motifs, and a new understanding of tribal insignia is thus needed.

The Khanates or principalities of Khiva and Bokhara prevailed until the 1860s. Enlisting the various Turkmen tribes as mercenaries, these rival principalities exploited the traditional tribal struggle for the richest grazing lands. The Salor and Saryk tribes were early victims of this conflict, and ceased to exist as tribal entities by the time the Tekke emerged as victors. Such tribal vicissitudes further complicate attribution of their rugs.

The ancient, self-sufficient, nomadic lifestyle of the Turkmen was severely disrupted by Russian Imperial expansion into the Transcaspian region. During the same period, Turkmen rugs became known and studied by outsiders. General Bogoliouboff, the Russian military governor of the Transcaspian Provinces, undertook the first scholarly work on Turkmen rugs in 1908.

The Russian takeover in the 1880s brought an increasing demand for tribal weavings, but with that demand came the inevitable effects on manufacture, such as the use of synthetic dyes and gradual commercialization which inevitably led to eventual mass production. In most cases, this resulted in a decline in craftsmanship: designs became simplified, guls more compressed, borders less elaborate, and colors harsher. Until these Turkmen tribes were incorporated into several Soviet Republics in the 1920s however, the weavers in the territories continued to produce outstanding examples of their traditional art.

The various tribes that had been known for centuries as the Salor, Saryk, Tekke, and Yomud, were nomadic wanderers who, in their generally westward movements, intermarried with Indo-Persian natives, settled down and adopted Islam. The Turkmen tribes were primarily herders of sheep, goats, and camels. Although portions of the tribes farmed, forming the settled group known as *chomur*, the majority belonged to the ruling *chovra*, or migratory element – fearless riders who indulged in an occasional raid, taking captives and holding them for ransom.

The women performed the household work, including rug weaving, although the men were in charge of dyeing the wool. As nomads valued these rugs highly, the prosperity of a family was often measured by the number of women engaged in making them.

The majority of 19th-century rugs were made for domestic use in the *kibitka* (tents). Edmond O'Donovan, a traveler in Merv in 1880, described the arrangement of these mostly small rugs:

The furniture of these tents (the dome-shaped wicker-hut, with its covering of reed mats and felt is very simple. The fire occupies the middle of the apartment, immediately under the central opening in the dome. The half of the floor remote from the entrance is covered with a ketche, or felt carpet, nearly an inch in thickness. On this are laid, here and there, Turkmen carpets, six or seven feet long by four to five in breadth, on which the inhabitants sit by day and sleep by night.... Round the walls hang large flat camel-bags, six feet by four, one side being entirely composed of the rich carpet-work in which the Turkmen women excel. Ordinarily, all the household goods are packed in these bags, for transit from place to place on the back of camels.

The most common formats of these household weavings, woven on small, portable looms include: torba, a long and narrow storage bag, usually sized 14-20 by 36-44 inches; chuval, a larger storage bag also used for bedding, 30-48 by 42-68 inches; khordjin, a saddlebag, 16-24 by 20-28 inches; tang, an external tent in a very long strip, 6-14 inches wide and up to 40-feet long; asmalik, a five-sided rug used as an animal trapping for wedding processions, 20-34 by 30-48 inches; ensi (pardah), a door hanging or prayer rug, usually in hatchli (cruciform) design, 48-60 by 60-84 inches; qalin, a floor covering or 'main carpet,' up to 5-7 by 11-12 feet.'

Some of these small weavings were produced using a variety of knotted and flatwoven techniques. The knotting varies between asymmetric and symmetric according to tribes: the Yomud and Sartyk use symmetric knots, but sometimes use some asymmetric knots in detailing.

Long kilim strips on the top and bottom ends are typical of these weavings. Wool and sometimes small amounts of silk or cotton are used. The warp and weft threads often contain a mixture of goat hair and wool, while the sides are frequently overcast with brown goat hair.

The color of Turkmen rugs is almost always madder red, in an endless variety of shades ranging from liver, oxblood, and brick red, to violet, brown, plum, chocolate, mahogany, and chestnut. A bright synthetic carmine known as 'Russian red' (Ponceau 2r) was introduced to Turkmen weavers along with other acid azo dyes between 1875 and 1880 and used at first in rather limited amounts. Indigo was used for blue, mostly in its darkest blue-black shade, or as a lovely light blue, found especially in earlier pieces. The limited use of yellow, green, and ivory highlights, and black or dark brown outlines would create subtle effects that alleviate color monotony.

The hatchli design seen in door hangings consists of a cruciform division of the field into four rectangular panels, usually filled with horizontal rows of Y-shaped motifs variously identified as shrubs, ram horns and bird heads. Occasionally, a small prayer arch, or a series of them, may be included at one end of the field, and as such, there is some opinion that these door hangings may have doubled as prayer rugs.

The most common Turkmen design uses a somewhat restricted vocabulary: a grid with octagonal or diamond-shaped major guls at the intersections, and other geometric devises, known as minor guls, in the spaces between. Originally, each tribe featured one or more highly specific insignia or gul, which were seen only on the large main carpets. When a tribe, such as the Salor, suffered defeat and disintegrated, the victorious group, such as the Tekke, they appropriated the emblems of the vanquished. Gradually various tribes borrowed and adapted the more popular or well-known guls, often simplifying them in the process.

The following classification by tribe applies mostly to the Turkmen rugs of the 19th century.

Traditionally regarded as the oldest and most distinguished Turkmen group, the Salor tribe is mentioned by Arab geographers as early as the 11th century. By the end of the 19th century, however, the tribe's numbers were dwindling, having suffered defeat with at the hands of the Tekkes.

Today a small group of Salor still exists near the town of Marutshak in Northern Afghanistan. Yet up to the mid 19th century, the Salor lived around Merv, and their distinctive gul is called the Merv or 'Mar' gul, identifiable by the small turret-like projections around its perimeter. Precision of drawing and finely articulated multiple narrow borders are characteristic of the best Salor rugs.

The Saryk tribe is often thought to be close relatives of the Salor as the two groups lived in close proximity to one another. Shortly after the downfall of the Salor in the 1850s, the Saryk too were forced to migrate South. Many of the tribe fled to Afghanistan, where they continued to make rugs in the Saryk manner. Structurally, these rugs are strongly associated with the use of the symmetric knot, though on later examples the asymmetric knot becomes more common. These weavings are also some of the most somber of the Turkmen rugs, the older Saryks being distinguished by a brown-purple tone. The gul most frequently associated with Saryk weaving is octagonal, containing a cross-like feature at the center with lobed ends. With Saryk weaving, however, one distinguishes the type not so much from the gul as from the color and the knotting.

Since the Tekke emerged as the dominant tribe in the 19th century, their rugs are the best known, having been exported to the West after the Russian conquest. So great a force they had become, that by 1963 there were reported to be some 300,000 Tekkes living around Merv.

Often the dividing line between Salor, Saryk, and Tekke is indistinct, because the former two tribes were partially absorbed by their conquerors. The Akhal Tekke lived around Ashkabad, now known as Ashgabat, the present-day capital of Turkmenistan, while other groups of Tekke lived to the East. The characteristic Tekke gul may be seen in a more rounded form in the earlier rugs. Unlike the many minor border stripes that characterize Saryk and Salor rugs, Tekke rugs have a major border usually repeating a radiating 'sunburst' rosette. A warm brick red is the most typical ground color, though a rich blood red can be seen in earlier examples.

The Tekke made large numbers of engsi in the hatchli design. Here, the ground color is a mellow abrashed medium red, and the main border of shrubs with serrated blue-and-white leaves carries over into the top panel of the skirt. The bottom panel often contains a lattice of eight-pointed flower heads on natural brown ground. The light blue and the generous, uncrowded spacing of the shrubs in the field are early features in this rug.

The widely dispersed Yomut tribe originally occupied Western Turkestan, especially the areas around Khiva and near the Caspian Sea. Due to the abundance of subgroups, such as the Goklan, Jafarbai, and Ogurdjali, there is great variation in characteristics, and a number of different guls – dyrnak, ertmen, kepse – are used.

Among the Yomut, the Turkish knot is more prevalent than the Persian knot, and the knotting is less fine than in other Turkmen groups, save for that of the Ersari. They favor liverish red, plum, light blue, yellow, and apricot (plate 196).

plate **196**
Yomut Turkmen Main Carpet
19th Century
6'2" x 10'6" (1.88 x 3.20m)
This rug highlights some of the finer aspects of Turkmen weavings. The crisply drawn kepse guls, derivatives of palmette figures from early floral rugs, are accentuated by a lively interplay of colors. A graceful movement is lent to the piece with the diagonal arrangement of colors, the muted apricot and blue guls giving rise to the more prominent indigo and white guls. The border belongs to an ancient family of curved meander or 'vine' borders, of which close parallels can be seen in some early Anatolian carpets. Often seen on Yomut rugs, it is commonly referred to as the 'boat' border.

Turkmen Rugs

A main carpet's feature is the Dyrnak gul. The light blue-green and apricot colors are effectively highlighted, and the variation in the small rectangular panels between the octagons of the main border indicates age, since later pieces show a more uniform treatment. The end panels contain handsome trees with multicolored serrated leaves bearing unique flower heads. The long kilim strips in red with narrow blue stripes complete the impression of considerable age conveyed by this harmonious rug. Later Yomud rugs, outstanding for fine and light weave, often seem custom-made for the European luxury market. The larger sizes feature elaborate borders and their colors cater to Western needs and tastes. The dark plum fields are enlivened by the brilliant cochineal red used in the guls.

The Chodor tribe was at one time identified with a subgroup of the Yomud. The two tribes share some guls, such as the ertmen, but Chodor rugs are quickly distinguished by their deep chocolate ground color.

The Ersari, one of the oldest recorded Turkmen groups on record, migrated in the 17th century from the Manguishlak district near the Caspian to the Bokhara region and down to Afghanistan. The subdivisions include the Chub-bash, the Beshire, and some Afghan tribes.

Some of the oldest surviving examples of Turkmen rugs belong to Ersari type (plate 199). Ersari rugs have the lightest and brightest colors of the Turkmen rugs, most frequently a cherry-red ground, with yellow, green, and light blue. Goat hair often constitutes at least a portion of the warp and weft. Ersari juvals in particular show the tribal preference for bright colors. Ersari (Beshire) prayer rugs are considered quite rare and are thus much sought-after by collectors.

Balouch rugs are produced by a number of tribes at various locations, mostly in the Khorasan province of Iran, Afghanistan, and Pakistan. Although many Persian and even Caucasian features occur in Balouch rugs, as a group they are most closely affiliated with the Turkmen. Balouch rugs usually come in smaller formats and contain a good deal of camel and goat hair in addition to wool. The color scheme of Balouch rugs is strongly associated to Turkmen weavings, with madder reds, indigo, and brown predominating, and a sparing use of white for borders and highlights. The Tree of Life design was very popular among the Balouch, and was often worked on a camel ground. This motif can be frequently seen on their small prayer rugs as well.

Flat-woven utility bags exemplify the kind of finely worked nomadic artifact that has become collectible recently. Good Balouch rugs are among the last authentic tribal pieces still generally available on the market for today's knowledgeable collector for reasonable prices (plates 197, 201, 202).

plate **197**
SARYK TORBA
1′5″ x 4′2″ (0.43 x 1.30m)

plate **198** | TURKMEN BAGFACE
19th Century
3′ x 4′ (0.91 x 1.22m)
*Woven by most Turkmen tribes,
flatwoven and pile woven juvals
with stripes often show designs
that are found on the borders of
other rugs. This large bag would
be used in the Turkmen yurt to
hold bedding and other
household items. During the
19th century these bags were
often woven with enormous care
and can sometimes rate among
the finest Turkmen weavings.*

plate **199** | Beshir Bukhara
7'7" x 17'7" (2.31 x 5.36m)
*An exemplary Beshir Bukhara
of the 19th century.*

plate **200**
Turkmen Saddle Cover
19th century
3′6″ x 4′6″ (1.07 x 1.37m)
Brilliant coloration on an
unusual ceremonial artefact.

plate **201** | Balouch

3′ x 6′ (0.91 x 1.83m)

*The antique Balouch illustrated
here has a distinctive design of
overall pattern with geometric
flowers set on unusual gold
background color with two
hands in two corners,
representing Panj Tan or five
Imams (Muslim saints).*

Turkmen Rugs

plate **202** | Balouch
3'3" x 6' (1.00 x 1.83m)
*Balouch tribal weaving are the
outskirts of Mashad and close to
Afghanistan border are very
collectable specially when
designs are a mixture of
geometric and floral patterns.*

Indian Rugs

If you ask an average rug dealer, collector or decorators about Kashmir rugs, they will respond by saying – Kashmir rugs are woven in Pakistan and they are late 20th century. The truth is, Kashmir was the first center of rug industry in India, starting in the 15th century. Scholars and the traders have always referred to these rugs as Mughal carpets.

The Mughals shared the Persian love of gardens. A descendent of both Timor and Genghis Khan, Babur (1483-1530), the first Mughal emperor, was famous for the gardens he designed and, as evidenced by miniature paintings of the time, often supervised the work himself.

Mughal rugs reflected this fascination with horticulture in their realistic presentations of flora and fauna, the like of which has not been seen in any other group of weavings. Trees, flowers, and wildlife are shown in extremely faithful renderings, so accurately drawn that the species may be identified. The extraordinarily fine knotting of these carpets made such precision possible. The colors were softer and lighter than their Persian counterparts, favoring a rich carmine pink. Prayer rugs in the millefleur style, hunting carpets, and fantastic animal-vegetable compositions were among the most typical products of the Mughal period.

Commercial records show that trade in 17th and 18th century Mughal carpets to Europe was extensive, at first controlled by the Portuguese, but eventually dominated by the British and Dutch. The majority of these early carpets show strong Persian influence, and depicts large floral, leaf and blossom figures on a red ground. The fields of these rugs were usually dyed with lac, an insect dye somewhat resembling cochineal but with its cooler, somewhat blueish tones.

Although the inspiration for early Indian rug design was largely Persian, the two styles may be distinguished with closer examination. In Indian rugs, natural forms are carefully and realistically depicted, whereas Persian weavers would transform these motifs into highly stylized forms. The rug art of India favors asymmetrical composition with great articulation of individual forms, while Persians tend toward symmetrical designs and a more subtle orchestration of them.

Classical Isfahan carpets of Persia were reproduced in exact design or reinterpreted versions in India during 16th and 17th centuries and continued into 19th century (plates 205, 206, 223).

Designs from other parts of Persia and other countries were reinterpreted during 19th century as well (plates 207, 208, 209, 214, 216, 218).

Not only Mughal Kings were speaking Persian and hiring Persian artisans. The British East India Company established its first carpet factory in 1611 at Masulipatnam, on Coromandel Coast, with Persian weavers. Persian artisans were already in Madras since 1550 according to some

records, not only as weavers, but also as merchants. They, together with the English, Dutch, Portuguese and French were engaged in international trade. Indian weavers have followed Persian designs with some variations through the centuries, with some minor differences in details. Even when the Master weaver chants in musical rhythm the colors to be woven by weavers, colors are called in Persian language, such as (Anari) Granet, which in Persian means Pomegranate red or Zard (Yellow). The type of knot used in Indian carpet is almost exclusively Persian knot (the asymmetrical knot).

The best example of Mughal rugs which most possibly were woven by Persian artisans is the fragment in the Altman Collection at the Metropolitan Museum of Art in New York, which has knot count of 2,516 per square inch (3,900,000 per square meter). This rug is of silk warp, weft and pile. For reasons yet unknown, rug production in India as well as Persia and Turkey came to a stand still in the 18th century. Very few examples of 18th century rugs are available to study. One reason could be imposition of several wars such as Nadir Shah, King of Persia's attack and Siege of Delhi in 1738, where he carried off to Persia the fabulous peacock throne of Shah Jahan and the distraction of the Ottomans of Turkey with their European engagements. These wars may have put a stop to the Court patronage of Royal weaving centers in all three important rug-producing countries of Middle East.

The Mughals' love of beauty and luxury resulted in the most splendid creations of the 17th century and many of the finest examples of Mughal carpets that have survived to the present day originate from the court workshops of Agra. Carpet workshops were introduced in Agra, the capital of the Mughal Empire for much of its history, in the early 17th century, when the country was under the reign of Akbar, Babur's grandson and the most celebrated of the empire's leaders. The name Agra was also sometimes assigned to the finer of Indian rugs made for export in the 19th century, although evidence that they were all made in Agra is scarce (plates 203, 204, 205, 211, 215, 219). It was also in Agra that the British East India Company was given a license by the court in 1612 to trade in India.

One of the most remarkable examples of Agra design, for 19th century is the asymmetrical composition of plate 205. Free in conception and brimming with life, pairs of winged creatures perch everywhere, in the grass and flowers on the ground, in the branches of bushes and trees. This detail provides an insight into the delicate sensitivity of these people, in whose eyes the couple is both the symbol of love, which motivates all creatures, and the origin of life.

Another important Agra carpet for the same period is illustrated in plate 212. The transitional design of this rug, especially the center medallion, recalls the Ardebil carpet from Victoria and Albert Museum of London. Its superimposed crosses and squares of unaffected style forms a motif with sixteen branches, drawn with palmettes at each point. These form a corona for the medallion, adding volume and pointing outwards in all directions.

Also prospering during the Mughal era was Lahore, located in
the Punjab region. Remnants of the splendors of that time are still visible
in the city's architecture. When British colonialism ended in 1947
and modern India and Pakistan were created, Lahore became part of
Pakistan, and has served as the country's cultural and intellectual capital
ever since.

Royal manufacturing of carpets, which had reached its peak of splen-
dor under the Mughals, declined after their dynasty fell. Rugs continued
to be made, but they were increasingly of an inferior quality. The subsequent colonization by the British resulted in the export of some of the
finest Indian rugs to England. Fortunately, this period was followed by a
revival in the 19th and 20th century, forming the basis for the Indian rugs
still available in the market.

The first major exhibition of these kind of carpets was held in
Crystal Palace, in London, in 1851, where 2 Kashmiri knotted rugs were
much appreciated. That exhibition supported by Indian Government and a
few British firms was the source of new inspiration for carpet waving of

276

Western firms and was followed by many books on the subject of Indian rugs. Notably: N.G. Mukerji (1907), H.T. Harris (1908), followed by Western Scholars, such as A&C Block of London (1900), K. Erdman of Germany (1966), and by important catalogue of M.S. Diamond on Oriental Rugs in Metropolitan Museum of Arts (1973).

Other centers of more recent production are Srinagar and Amritsar, where many fine 19th-century examples originated. Amritsar, which literally means, the Lake of Immortality, is the spiritual home of the Sikh religion and the principal city of the Punjab region (plates 210, 213, 217). Production began in volume in 1809, when the Maharaja Ranjit Singh encouraged the recruitment of shawl weavers from Kashmir. The city's glory as the center of India's rug production was short-lived, as the increased demand from Europe and the United States led to mass production and lower quality; from 1898 on Amritser produced a large number of poorly made and poorly dyed rugs.

In the early 20th century, with some workshops that were of notable exception, India began to export large numbers of rugs of generally lesser quality that were mostly reproductions of Persian designs. This was a response to increased demand from Europe and the United States, as well as a way to employ thousands of weavers whose skills were no longer needed when the 'Kashmir Shawl' lost favor in European fashion capitals. Also at this time, the British colonialists introduced commercial production by prison labor in towns such as Bangalore and Mirzapur. These large, heavy pieces were sometimes coarse and of such low grade that at one time they were not allowed into the United States. Ironically, some of the finest Agra carpets are ascribed to prison production by some sources. Since designs were copied from old books, catalogues, and museum rugs, there is no way to know which rugs were produced in the jails, and which came from the town centers. Flat woven all cotton Dhurry rugs were also produced in the 19th and 20th century, some of them with superior quality (plate 220, 221).

Actually, Indian carpets were not in very great demand by the European trading companies, their designs leaving something to be desired from the perspective of Western taste. Moreover, the weaving centers worked primarily for the Mughal court, as well as, later on, for the other Indian courts. In addition, the inordinate amount of time that it took to weave the carpets, worked against the quick profit in the interest of which the trading companies' agents would sometimes compromise on the quality of the goods they dispatched to the West. Taken together, these factors did not provide much incentive to produce for Europe, where Indian rugs arrived mainly as diplomatic gift. Great Britain's East India Company preferred to place its orders for Oriental carpets with the workshops of Persia, which could supply high-quality pieces much more rapidly.

plate **205** | Agra Rug
Early 19th Century
based on 16th century Mughal
8'10" x 11'10" (2.69 x 3.60m)
This carpet design is remarkable by the asymmetrical composition, freer in conception and brimming with life.
Pairs of winged creatures perch everywhere, in the grass and flowers on the ground, in the branches of bushes and trees. This detail provides an insight into the delicate sensitivity of these people, in whose eyes the couple is both the symbol of love, which motivates all creatures, and the origin of life. The coloring of the flowers and leaves and the predominantly beige plumage of the birds are highlighted perfectly by the blood-red ground – the whole carpet is a celebration of life, tenderness and elegance.
The clarity and sequence of the motifs in the border provide a very fitting frame: palmettes containing animal masks run between two golden guard bands dotted with flowers.

Indian Rugs

plate **206** | INDO-ISFAHAN CARPET
19th century
11'3" x 16' (3.43 x 4.88m)
This carpet is woven in Northern India but uses Persian Safavid period carpets for its inspiration. The theme is that of a paradise park which symbolizes Persian idea of what the heavenly domain would be like. The cypress trees, peacocks amidst scrolling vines are found in many period carpets of the time. The medallion, the pendants flowing from it and the reciprical crown design of the border are very similar in form to the famous medallion and animal carpet in Prince Scwarzenberg's collection in Vienna. This carpet mimics the elegance of the latter yet has a truly Indian feel to it in the manner of it color and drawing. A masterpiece of a more recent era.

Indian Rugs

plate **207** | INDIAN CARPET
19th century
17′ x 28′ (5.18 x 8.53m)

The design of many Kerman and North Indian carpets is similar due to the close trade relations between these two areas. Therefore it is not unusual to find a Kerman rug design used in Indian carpets. The light colors and silky wool add a subtle texture to the lattice made up of biaxailly reflected in cartouches. The graceful movement of the total design is created by simple yet subtle color harmonies changes in color.

plate **208** | SOUTH INDIAN RUG
9'9" x 13'9" (2.97 x 4.19m)
Adaptation of Dorokash design of Iran with some changes of the borders design and complete change of colors, makes this rug distinguishable from Persian rugs.

plate **209** | SOUTH INDIAN RUG
19th Century
9'4" x 14' (2.84 x 4.272m)
Both Caucasian and Persian influences can be seen in the idiosyncratic design of this rug. The medallions flanking the inner border are clearly derived from those of early garden carpets while the geometric composition gives this rug a Caucasian quality. The rosettes in the minor borders add an elegance that balances the energetic drawing of the field.

Indian Rugs

plate **210** | Amritsar Carpet
19th Century
11'4" x 13'5" (3.45 x 4.09m)
This carpet shows the popular Amritsar golden ground. The elegant Persian border reflects perhaps the most notable skill of Indian weavers – the ability to take Persian designs and recreate them with a very realistic interpretation.

plate **211** | Agra Carpet
19th Century
11′8″ x 13′7″ (3.56 x 4.14m)
The delicate drawing and the refined use of colors in this Agra represent the best of Indian carpet weaving during the 19th century. The classical Mughal design is rendered with exquisite artistry, while the use of green and lac red as the two primary colors invests the carpet with a noble elegance.

Indian Rugs

plate **212** | AGRA CARPET
19th Century
9′ x 12′ (2.74 x 3.66m)
*The transitional design of this
rug, especially the center
medallion, recalls the Ardebil
carpet from Victoria and Albert
Museum of London. Its
superimposed crosses and
squares of unaffected style
forms a motif with sixteen
branches, drawn with palmettes
at each point. These form a
corona for the medallion, adding
volume and pointing outwards
in all directions.*
*Another unusual feature is that
the stylized flowers of the
medallion do not grow from
vases in the middle of the
borders but from standing or
hanging oil-lamps. The designer
must have wanted the center of
the carpet to be a theatre of light
rather than a floral
arrangement.*
*The border is a sequence of
medallion: large-scale ones in
red, the smaller ones in white
framing a device rather like a
Maltese cross.*

plate **213** | Amritsar Carpet
19th Century
12′ x 15′ (3.66 x 4.57m)
This carpet has many qualities that lend it a collectible appeal. The design resembles to two multiple prayer rugs, with the mihrabs (prayer arches) connecting through the middle of the carpet. The line of rosettes running through the center of the carpet reinforces this idea by urging the eye to divide the field. The mihrabs themselves are drawn in a similar fashion to those found on Turkish Kula prayer rugs. A beautiful carpet, in perfect decorative dimensions.

Indian Rugs

plate **214** | Indo Tabriz

15′ x 27′ (4.57 x 8.23m)
*This is early 20th century
adaptation of older Persian
design, mostly from Tabriz area.
An enormous size, the larger
scale flowers executed are quite
elaborate. The colors are local,
the design borrowed.*

plate **215** | Agra Carpet
19th century
3'10" x 6'8" (1.17 x 2.03m)
*Vigorously geometric and
angular, the drawing of this rug
gives it a strong Caucasian
character. The carpet illustrates
the extraordinary talent of 19th
century Indian weavers in
replicating the designs of other
weaving repertoires. The colors
also typify those found on rugs
of the Caucasian tradition.*

Indian Rugs

plate **216** | Indo-Tabriz
11' x 15'9" (3.31 x 4.8m)
Based on a 17th century rug of
Northwest Persia. On a dark
blue field spiral scrolls with
arabesque, flowered and almost
angular bands with colors of
green peach and soft blue create
a well balanced design. Since the
field design is so elegant, the
border is less noticeable and
more complimentary.

plate **217** | Amritsar
19th century
14' x 16' (4.27 x 4.88m)
*At first glance you will think
that this is an Ushak carpet, but
closer examination of the weave
and structure it becomes obvious
that this is woven in Amritsar
India.*

Indian Rugs

plate **219** | Agra Carpet
Early 20th century
6′ x 8′6″ (1.83 x 2.59m)
A beautifully drawn carpet, the
extremely fine detail of its
central medallion and the
surrounding field become more
compelling to the eye the longer
one looks at it. A veritable work
of art.

Indian Rugs

plate **220** | Dhurrie
19th century
4'7" x 7'5" (1.40 x 2.26m)
This superb example of cotton Dhurrie, probably made for an Indian summer palace, is a unique artistic representation of outdoor life in the palace. The naturalistic representation of animal figures on an architecturally designed foreground together with the great harmony of colors makes this masterpiece an outstanding example.

plate **221** | DHURRY

12′10″ x 13′8″ (3.91 x 4.17m)
*The very fine weave of this
carpet allows the overall repeat
design to work so successfully, as
does the bold 'Greek key' style
border which powerfully frames
the field of geometric flowers in
very elegant setting. The use of
differing shades of blue
throughout lends movement to
the drawing and gives the rug a
very subtle and fresh quality.*

plate **222** | AGRA CARPET
19th century
4′ x 7′ (1.22 x 2.13m)
*An oatmeal colored ground
shows how elegantly some of
the Indian rugs of the 19th
century interpreted Persian
design motifs, in this case, the
Herati.*

Indian Rugs

plate **223** | EAST INDIAN CARPET
Early 19th century
3′6″ x 6′ (1.07 x 1.83m)
*This rug is an enigma as it has
the characteristics of Isfahan,
Indian, Kurdish and Herat
weavings. The design is typical of
the early Herat carpets exported
to the West at the beginning of
the 19th century. The scale of the
border and the field design speak
of a pre-Revival date, before
1865, for this striking carpet.*

Chinese Rugs

The rugs of China and East Turkestan form a unique group among Oriental rugs. The designs on these rugs are both striking for their simplicity and harmonious compositions, easily distinguished by Western eyes through their association with Chinese porcelains and paintings, and for their elegant and restrained use of color. The elaborate and explicit vocabulary of symbols, meticulously employed, adds a fascinating layer of meaning to the designs. Many of these motifs are thought to predate the art of commercial rug-making in China; thirteenth-century Chinese paintings depict Mongol rather than Chinese rugs, and no Chinese pile rugs can be dated with absolute certainty to before the 17th century.

While there is no particular evidence that points to the rug weaving tradition in China as a major art form, written references mention trade in carpets as early as the first century AD. During the T'ang period (618-907), Chinese Buddhists observed the use of carpets in the course of their pilgrimages across China to India. More telling, in 756, a group of 31 felt rugs were donated to the Shosoin Treasury in Nara, Japan, catalogued as Chinese. The designs on many of these rugs include very classical Chinese symbols, including clouds and lotus blossoms.

By the period of the Yuan Dynasty (1271-1368) and the Mongol conquest, there are more detailed literary references to carpets in China, though whether or not these were to pile carpets remains uncertain. We know unequivocally, however, that the Mongol invaders were familiar with pile weaving, and there is no reason to think that they didn't bring the tradition with them to China.

In the succeeding Ming dynasty (1368-1644), there is a similar paucity of references or evidence that would help us date surviving rugs from that period, although some scholars point to the 'ancestor paintings' from that time, which include images of carpets. These depictions have been likened to various rugs on the market over the years in attempts to date them, and as such there are now rugs catalogued as 17th century, Ming period.

The most conclusive documentation of 17th century weaving comes with the arrival of the Manchus, just before the end of the Ming period. Jesuit missionaries record the presence of fine carpets in the courts of Emperor K'ang Hsi. During the 17th century we also find two references to Chinese carpets in English inventories, though none detailed enough to confirm that these weavings were of a Chinese production.

There is a similar amount of uncertainty regarding the origins of carpet weaving in China. The practice was most likely first introduced to China through the Eastern section of the great plateau known as Chinese Turkestan, often generally referred to as Xinkiang province. Having been under Chinese jurisdiction intermittently since the Han period (206 BC - 220 AD), it is populated by a mixed ethnic people, united by a common language known as Jagatai Turkish. These semi-nomadic groups settled in oasis towns, the best known of which are those around the Takla Makan desert: Kashgar, Khotan, and Yarkand.

The exceedingly dry, hot climate of the region helped to preserve archaeological evidence of an early weaving production. We know from rug fragments discovered by A. LeCoq and Sir Aurel Stein that the people of East Turkestan have made rugs since at least the 3rd century.

Rugs from East Turkestan have a very unique sensibility; their design repertoire, colors and motifs bear little resemblance to those rugs we traditionally associate with Chinese production. This might well have to do with the fact that the indigenous population of East Turkestan is Muslim, and consequently their rugs show more likeness to West and Central Asian weavings.

More recently made rugs in the Tarim Basin in the Northern province of Xinkiang rarely appear on the market. They come from the oasis cities of Samarkand, Yarkand, Kashgar, and Khotan, although the German writer Hans Bidder believes most were produced at Khotan (plate 235).

The palette of these rugs is often lighter than that in Chinese rugs, with red, yellow, and blue used predominantly. The Turkestan weavers often use silk or metallic threads, especially in Kashgar pieces, and these rugs evince as much Persian influence as Chinese. The most common design is the disk medallion. The pomegranate and vase, the boxed chrysanthemum gul, and overall patterns such as the *Herati* often occur in East Turkestan rugs. Occasionally, one finds multiple prayer rugs (*saphs*) emulating the popular Turkmen prayer-rug type.

Most early rugs were woven in the Northern Chinese wool belt where wool was abundant, although some were produced in the South. The four Northern provinces particularly active in the weaving industry were Ningxia, Suiyuan, Chadhar, and Jehol. Important centers also developed along the two great rivers of China which served as the main thoroughfares of communication: Lanchow, Paotoa, Kalgan, Jehol, and Shanhaikuan on the Hang Ho River, and Hankow, Nanking, and Shanghai on the Yangtze Kiang River.

The prevailing tendency to copy older styles was carried to an extreme in China, and has further complicated precise dating of Chinese rugs. Scholars including H. A. Lorentz, David Wang, and Murray Eiland among others have traced their development largely through the use of particular colors and patterns, as well as by their technical features. While there are distinct styles within each area, they have not yet been sufficiently studied to allow for categorization of the rugs according to region. For the moment, it is more reasonable to group them by period.

The few extant rugs now dated to the 17th-century Ming dynasty show finely drawn and elaborate dragon and phoenix designs, such as that seen in the rug often referred to simply as the 'Chinese Fragment,' in the collection of the Metropolitan Museum of Art, New York. A fine piece reflecting the ancient style, it has a restricted palette of dark brown floral sprigs meandering on a field of deep gold, surrounded by an inner strip of light blue and an outer border of traditional swastikas in an endless chain. Characteristic of the rugs dated to this period are palettes of warm, yet corrosive red-browns and yellows, dark indigos and a single shade of blue; the presence of very narrow, simple borders; and, perhaps most notably, an elegant, beautifully rendered curvilinear drawing achieved in part by the use of half knots. Also typical of the group is a very course weave, sometimes as low as 15 knots per square inch.

The 18th century, known as the Ch'ien Lung period, marked the appearance of several new colors, such as light blue, peach, and fawn, along with delicately drawn floral elements, peony borders, and medallions. Overall diaper and fret patterns were also popular around this time. In medallion designs, four quartered medallions may appear in the corners or spandrels of the field design in addition to the single central medallion. In general, the Ch'ien Lung period may be considered the renaissance of Chinese rug weaving. Many of the 18th-century characteristics described above also occur in rugs woven in the 19th century (plates 224, 236).

By the 19th century, in addition to madder reds and golds ranging from carmine to amber, a peach blush tint was achieved by dyeing first with yellow, then with madder. At the same time, quieter and more sparsely decorated rugs were being made, typified by open fields and a few scattered floral ornaments surrounding the central medallion. These rugs prove that these noble and somewhat austere compositions continued to be favored throughout the 19th century (plates 229, 230, 233, 237).

By the second half of the 19th century, China became fully open to Western trade. New workshops sprang up in Peking, Tientsin, and Ningxia. In trade, only two basic distinctions were made in rugs: Ningxia denoted any piece of quality, while any long pile piece was called Peking. Around the turn of the century, the introduction of aniline dyes led to the presence of garish, severe colors in greens, pinks, and golds. Traditional designs of

Chinese Rugs

plate **224**

CHINESE THRONE BACK COVER
Mid 19th century
2'2" x 2'5" (0.66 x 0.74m)
*On this superb piece, shaped to
fit the back of a throne or chair,
two Fu-lions appear, with
various Buddhist symbols
scattered in the field around
them. These include the conch
shell, fish, covered vase, and
endless knot. The lower border
displays the classic design of a
mountain rising from the sea; a
graceful floral pattern decorates
the remaining border area.*

dragons and florals increased in size to fill the field of the whole rug. The average size of rugs increased also, to accommodate large Western homes, and Western demand for 'bedroom sets', two runners and a large carpet, also elicited an increased production in this format (plates 227, 228, 230, 231, 233).

With the introduction of improved synthetic dyes deep purple, lilac, jade, and wine-red colors were used in a series of dynamic Art Deco inspired rugs were created in the early 20th century (plates 225, 226).

Apart from the traditional palace and temple floor coverings, the Chinese often preferred scatter rugs for furniture coverings and bedding (plate 224). Special formats included scalloped seat covers and saddle rugs, as well as circular rugs. Room-size rugs were mostly designed for Western markets.

Technically, Chinese rugs do not compare with the fine weave and suppleness of Persian and Turkmen rugs. They are usually quite coarsely knotted with the symmetric knots. This construction is ideally suited to the compositional themes of spacious fields scattered with large scale ornamentation.

Sheep's wool, originally not produced in China proper in any quantity, came in abundance from Mongolia through trade with the nomads.

plate **225** | Chinese Carpet
Circa 1920
8'11" x 11'9" (2.72 x 3.58m)
*Made in Northwest China at the
beginning of the 19th century,
this carpet typifies the Chinese
Art Deco style of carpet weaving
that was successfully retailed
through some of the major
department stores in the West.
The drawing is both spacious
and refined with an almost
complete lack of ornamentation
in the borders.*

Tibet provided wool of the best quality, along with goat and yak hair. Camel wool was mostly reserved for some of the beautiful beige and ivory tones in Chinese rugs. Rugs woven for special occasions called for silk and metallic threads. The warp of Chinese rugs is almost invariably cotton.

Unlike most other types of Oriental rugs, Chinese rugs convey quite specific messages with their decorative symbols. These often ancient conventions were readily legible to an educated audience within the cultural framework that produced them, but interpretation is needed for the Western viewer. All aspects of Chinese tradition – Taoist, Confucian, and Buddhist – appear and sometimes overlap in these weavings. The use of a number of different motifs from different traditions can often be evidence of a later weaving, where their inclusion was not necessarily to convey symbolic meaning but rather to appeal to the Western appetite for such elements.

It must be noted that the meanings described here are simplifications of profound philosophical beliefs and are subject to varied interpretations.

One of the most universal of these ancient symbols is the swastika, or hooked cross. It symbolizes 'good luck' if used on its own, and 'ten-

plate **226** | CHINESE CARPET
Circa 1920
9' x 12' (2.74 x 3.66m)
The plum colored field of this Art Deco carpet creates an appropriate background for the profusion of floral elements that fluorish throughout the field. Woven at the peak of commercial production, this carpet still retains the charm and elegance of older weavings.

thousandfold happiness' if repeated in an endless diaper pattern or fretwork border. The 'pearl' border and the 'T' and 'key' patterns all originated in equally distant times, indeed their designs can be seen on the earliest Chinese bronze ceremonial objects.

Another fundamental symbol of great antiquity, the 'yin-yang' motif represents the interlocking, inseparable duality of male and female, dark and light, cold and warmth.

Sometimes the yin-yang motifs forms the center of a medallion and is surrounded by the 'Eight Trigrams' (*pa-kua*). These combinations of broken and unbroken lines form sub-units of the hexagrams in the *I-Ching*, and different arrangements have different meanings: heaven, wind, earth, fire, water, mountain, thunder, or clouds.

The elements of nature – water, cloud, mountain, fire – play an important role in the symbology of the *I-Ching* and frequently appear on Chinese rugs in conventionalized form. Calm water is often denoted by semicircles, and rough water, by squarish or triangular shapes, often combined with concentric scalloped triangles that signify mountain and rock. Occasionally, small dots or cloud shapes suggest sea foam. Lightning and fire similarly take on stylized abbreviations.

Another variation of the form is seen in later uses of yin-yang symbol, which often stylistically combine the characters for *shou, fu* and double *hsi*. The Chinese character *shou* denotes long life, the equally auspicious *fu*, good luck, (also the word for bat, another popular motif), while the double *hsi* represents wedded bliss.

The use of mythical creatures in Chinese weaving adds yet another layer of symbolic language. Chief among them is the dragon, which exudes entirely different qualities than its more menacing Western counterpart. In Chinese art, the dragon symbolizes the supreme majesty of nature and its driving energy. Translated into the human sphere, the five-clawed dragon relates to the emperor (plate 232).

The phoenix (*feng-huang*), typically seen as a hybrid pheasant, peacock, and crane, often represents the Empress. Unicorns (*ch'i lin*) combine the head of a dragon, the body of a stag, the tail of an ox, and the hooves of a horse. Flying through the sky with flames rising from its shoulders, the unicorn lives a thousand years and appears at the birth of sages. Fu-dogs (*shitzu*) resemble lions, and are the reputed guardians of Buddhist sacred places.

Animals seen in Chinese rugs may also denote the twelve sectors of the ancient Chinese zodiac: horse, dog, steer, monkey, serpent, dragon, rabbit, rat, tiger, hare, fowl, and boar. Storks and cranes symbolize old age and longevity, horses nobility, and fishes abundance. Butterflies are a rebus for long life. Animals can also be used to express the hours of the day.

The consummate floral symbol, the lotus, rising from muddy waters, conveys the purity of the divine. The chrysanthemum and peony, together with the narcissus, are emblems of constancy and wealth, and together they complete the four flowers of the seasons. The peach is the most auspicious fruit, followed in popularity by the pomegranate, the paragon of

Chinese Rugs

fertility. Chinese artists also favored the lime because of the resemblance of its rinds to the hands of a reposing Buddha.

At times, pictorial rugs carry entire groups of symbols, such as the Buddhist eight emblems: wheel of the law, conch shell, state umbrella, canopy, lotus, covered vase, pair of fishes, and endless knot. Or they may use the eight symbols of Taoism: fan, sword, staff and gourd, castanets, baskets of flowers, flute, bamboo, and lotus pod.

It follows that such a rich array of symbolic ornament served ceremonial and ritual functions. For instance the column or pillar rug was often woven without borders so that when it was wrapped around the temple or palace pillars, its sides met and the composition became complete. A very unusual representative of this group shows a five-clawed dragon with its head at one end and its backbone running down the middle of the rug. The other end of the rug contains a conventional wave-foam-rock configuration (plate 232).

plate **227** | Chinese Carpet
19th century
13'3" x 19'8" (4.04 x 6.00m)

*These blue-field 'Peking' rugs
had become immensely popular
by the early 20th century,
considered the height of vogue
in Western interior design.
The carpet is lent a joyous
movement by the presence of
fluttering birds and the cloud-
encircled medallions, while the
overall composition is lifted and
rendered complete by the
various Buddhist emblems of
happy augury which punctuate
the deep blue field.*

Chinese Rugs

plate **228** | CHINESE CARPET
19th century (2.82 x 3.53m)
9'3" x 11'7"
The appeal of this rug lies in the
dense drawing of its central field
and its almost painterly
sensibility, with a plethora of
scenic arrangements and a
veritable overgrowth of flora,
fauna and emblems crowding
the intense blue ground. The
simple border amply frames the
carpet's elaborate interior, and
balances the overall composition
of the carpet.

plate **229** | CHINESE CARPET
19th century
7'9" x 9'9" (2.36 x 2.97m)
*Both the colors and exquisite
drawing in this carpet evoke
tremendous feeling of serenity.
The sparse, somewhat minimal
field is given life by the
ornamentation of the spandrels
and the central medallion, with
the presence of very finely
drawn stags and peacocks. The
subtle interplay of the differing
shades of blue add further
dimension to this magnificent
carpet.*

Chinese Rugs

plate **230** | Chinese Carpet
19th century
9'2" x 11'9" (2.79 x 3.58m)
Another exquisite example of a
'Peking' rug, the real essence of
this carpet lies in the main
border. The harmonious placing
of the pagodas in each of the
four corners and the flight of
birds against a midnight blue
background warm the entire rug.
A very dignified, subtle carpet of
great decorative value.

plate **231** | Chinese Carpet
19th century
6′2″ x 8′7″ (1.88 x 2.62m)
*A delicately colored piece of the
Ningshia type, this rug has
lustrous wool and an extremely
graceful drawing. The outer
pearl border finishes the piece
with a certain charm and
playfulness.*

Chinese Rugs

plate **232**
CHINESE COLUMN RUGS
(One of a Pair)
19th century
4'4" x 8'8" (1.32 x 2.64m)
*Rugs of this type were made to
fit around the columns of
temples and palaces. The lack of
side borders allowed the design
to complete itself once wrapped
around the pillar. Here we see
the five-clawed dragon chasing
the Pearl of Eternity*

plate **233** | CHINESE CARPET
Circa 1900
6′9″ x 14′7″ (2.06 x 4.45m)
This rug has a startling elegance, epitomised by the restrained and delicate drawing of the central medallion and spandrels. The muted palette allows the freshness and fineness of the drawing to shine.

plate **234** | Mongolian Carpet
20th century
12′6 x 14′6″ (3.81 x 4.50m)
The Greek key design border is
of such grand scale and bold
excution that it dominates the
field that uses a fret design
interspersed by flowers.

*The coloring is not typical of
these carpets, which were made
in workshops set up by the
Chinese for export weaving. The
scale and breadth of the whole
composition make this carpet a
masterpiece.*

plate **235** | Khotan Rug
Early 19th century
3′9″ x 7′9″ (1.14 x 2.36m)
Although slightly worn the majestic design of this carpet is still very apparent. The two vase issuing flowering pomegranate stems is one of the designs popular with these oasis city weavers. The medallion incorprated into this design is rare as is the bilateral symmetry of the composition.

Chinese Rugs

plate **236** | Chinese Carpet
Circa 1800
2′ x 4′3″ (0.61 x 1.30m)
The subtle colours belie the exuberance of the design in this early carpet. The sophistication of the design is epitomised in the central medallion and the clever use of different colors to add a third dimension to the carpet. Like many rugs, the more one looks at this piece, the more wondrous it becomes.

plate **237** | CHINESE
20th century
15′8″ x 16′4″ (4.78 x 4.98m)
Tientsin rug of 19th century,
large open field and medallion
are surrounded with floral
symbols. Outstanding border
with many Chinese decorations.
The Blackish Gray background,
almost like Corommandel
screens of the same period, is
really unique.

Chinese Rugs

European Rugs

When the sumptuous carpets of the East arrived on the Continent with the returning Crusaders, Europeans were most impressed by their luxurious textures and dazzling colors. We know from the paintings of the time that Turkish carpets became much admired at the court of King Henry VIII. Royalty and the nobility were frequently painted standing on a carpet, which was considered a powerful symbol of their wealth and worldliness. Frequently, carpets were considered so valuable and rare that their use was limited to table covers – as often seen in the 16th-century paintings of Hans Holbein The Younger (1497-1543). A number of works by this artist, who worked in King Henry's court, depict known types of early Turkish weaving. However, it was not only at the court that these works of art were admired. In *Georg Gisze, a German merchant in London,* Holbein shows his subject surrounded by the trappings of his profession, including a type of carpet from West Anatolia that can still occasionally be found on the market today.

As soon as these carpets began to arrive in the West, Europeans began to set up their own manufactories. Pile weavings were made that were often in imitation of their oriental prototypes – in the 17th century, such pieces were often referred to as 'Turkey work', an acknowledgement of the huge influence of that country on European production.

It was not until the beginning of the 18th century that Europeans other than the Spanish began to produce their own room-size carpets in significant quantities for use on the floor. Virtually every country in Europe has produced rugs: France, England, Spain, Germany, Scandinavia, Belgium, Poland, Greece, and Portugal all have their own distinctive traditions. Here we will discuss only those countries whose weaving culture left an indelible mark on the history of the carpet or those who produced carpets in significant quantities.

Spain

Hispania, as the Iberian Peninsula was called, was part of the Roman Empire, as were the countries of France, England, and Italy. In the 5th century, Christian armies of warriors, the Visigoths, swept down from the Northern Europe, destroying everything in sight. Many remained in this expansive peninsula as farmers. Later, the Moors, Islamic invaders from North Africa drove the Visigoths back and firmly established a centralized and powerful presence in Southern Spain, modern day Andalusia, under which arts and crafts flourished. The new rulers were called Saracens (people of the desert) and were a polyglot of Arabs, Syrians, Egyptians, and Berbers, who brought with them elements from civilizations throughout the Islamic world. They had encountered the luxuries of Persia and Asia Minor and sought to mimic the courts of the East with their own ateliers and craftsmen. These court artists were skilled in a variety of media – carpets, textiles, the arts of the book, mosaic work, metalwork, ceramics, and architecture.

The city of Cordoba was established in 756 and became the Islamic capital of Spain. It was second only to Constantinople in size and importance in the Islamic world. The Moors called it 'the Bride of Andalusia'. The Moores remained powerful until the 9th century when Charlemagne (King Charles I of France) drove them to the heart of Andalusia, where they remained until their expulsion in 1492.

The important and highly influential Spanish rug industry which had been established by the Moors continued to flourish under Christian rule. The main centers of rug production were at Chinchilla, Leturi, Alcaraz, and Mudejar, which created a distinctive style of rug from the fusion of Moorish and Western design. Mudejar, the name given to Muslims living in Spain under Christain rule, rugs are arguably the only Western carpets that have incorporated Western and Islamic design with perfect harmony, and the design of these carpets later influenced Spain's famous 'heraldic' rugs.

The city of Alcaraz is situated between Granada and Cuenca and is mentioned in many historical documents, especially those of the 16th and 17th centuries, during which time Cuenca was a prosperous center with important carpet manufactories, producing rugs inspired by contemporary Turkish designs. A few surviving examples from Cuenca and Alcaraz remind us of the mastery of Spanish carpet weaving (plate 241).

To the North, the French had been developing a style of carpet that was entirely different from the Islamic tradition in Spain. Perhaps eager to draw a line underneath his country's Islamic past, King Philip XV (1683-1746) set up a royal factory in Madrid. Initially, this workshop produced only tapestries and flat-woven carpets, but soon pile-woven carpets were made in imitation of the so-called 'Savonnerie' carpets in France. Spain's oriental designs slowly died out, and by the 19th century, factories were influenced by France's hugely successful carpets, although the Spanish tended to favor lighter colors than those used by the French (plate 242).

Sadly, Spain's prestigious weaving tradition, arguably the richest in all Europe, came to an end towards the middle of the last century. After the outbreak of the Spanish Civil War in 1936, the output of the royal looms – such as those at Madrid – rapidly diminished. The famed Spanish needle-point industry, which briefly outshone the country's carpet making of the early 20th century, was largely surpassed by Portugal (plate 255).

France

The first rugs of importance to appear in France were those brought in by Louis IX (Saint Louis) on return from his crusade to Palestine in 1254. The French referred to them as Saracens, and it is thought that from that time, French nobles produced their own rugs and tapestries to decorate their tents or shelters when abroad. These Saracenic rugs initiated a taste for novel floor and furniture coverings. Since these elevated beginnings, France has supported the artists who produce tapestries, carpets, and home furnishing more than any other European country.

The two principal types of floor covering produced in France are known as Aubussons and Savonneries; both have a style that has come to recognize as uniquely French. Aubusson rugs are mostly flat woven, while Savonneries are always pile woven. Both types were almost exclusively made for the aristocracy until the 19th century, when production increased to serve a wider audience.

Under the reign of Henry IV (1553-1610), a court atelier was established at the Louvre, where skilled artisans were commissioned to produce furniture, bronzes and carpets for use by the King. The first carpets produced at this time were apparently copies of oriental designs using the Turkish knot.

Under Louis XIV, carpet production increased dramatically, and in 1644 it was decided to move the carpet weavers to a former soap factory (*Savonnerie*) in the village of Chaillot, just outside Paris. Pierre Dupont, a former illuminator, obtained license from the King to co-fond the new Savonnerie workshop with Simon Lourdet. Dupont proceeded to study the art of Turkish rug-making, actually travelling to Constantinople to carry out research.

A 1653 inventory list of Cardinal Magarine, Prime Minister to Louis XIV, describes in detail 21 Persian carpets, six Turkish carpets, and only one Savonnerie carpet in the King's collection. However, the list also contains information about a group of Savonnerie carpets produced as gifts to be presented to foreign ambassadors, and we know that Dupont and Lourdet wove a group of 13 brown-ground carpets for use in the Galerie d'Apollon and the Grande Galerie in the Louvre.

Savonneries came in a variety of patterns to suit the tastes of the age, favoring popular baroque and rococo motifs, as well as pastoral and historic scenes. A palace-size rug illustrates the architectural framing and paneling devices used, imitating gilt *boiseries* and brocades enriched with bouquets of flowers in full bloom. Most of the antique Savonnerie carpets that appear on the market today originate from the second half of the first Empire and from the Barbour restoration period. Many were designed by an artist known as Saint-Ange (1780-1860) (plate 244).

The French revolution was disastrous for the carpet business and in 1826 the Gobelin tapestry workshop and Savonnerie carpet workshops were housed together in the Gobelin atelier. There, near Paris, they still make carpets. The finest Gobelin weaving was done for the French court with cartoons inspired by the artist decorator, Charles Lebrun. Today, a school and a museum are attached to the current workshop.

The Aubusson workshop, located in the Creuse Valley, rivaled the Savonnerie, and its rugs followed the same historical trends as the Savonnerie. LeBrun and other famous painters were commissioned to provide designs.

By the mid-18th century, there was an increased demand for floor carpets by the nobility and court of Louis XV. This, combined with the extremely depressed conditions in Aubusson and the nearby village of Felletin, brought about a local economy based almost entirely on the production of pile- and flat-woven (tapestry woven) carpets (plates 246, 248, 249, 250).

The Beauvais Royal Manufactory was established in 1664 by Colbert to weave tapestries for hanging and upholstery. In 1780 De Menza, a former tapestry and carpet manufacturer in Aubusson, was appointed director of the Beauvais workshop. In this position, which he held for 12 years, he oversaw the production of some pile- and flat-woven floor carpets. These bear close resemblance to the 18th century weavings of Aubusson, although the latter are still distinguishable by their finer weave and superior colors. Many of these carpets have BEAUVAIS written into the design on the outer border. Beauvais closed in 1793, after the French Revolution, but reopened the following year under state sponsorship. In 1940, it was forced to move to the Gobelin building as well.

England

The earliest known interest in rug weaving in England began when Eleanor of Castile, Spanish bride of Edward I, brought a large selection of Moorish rugs to England in the 13th century. Their beauty astonished the English Royalty and their guests, but the country did not manufacture any rugs until in the following century. Edward III encouraged weaving in the 14th century by inviting Flemish craftsmen to settle in England.

By the 16th century, rugs had become status symbols, items of great prestige amongst the affluent. In 1520 Cardinal Wolsey is recorded as having acquired more than 60 rugs from Venetian trade merchants, a sure sign of the growing allure of the Oriental rug.

By the 17th century, English royalty had established factories to rival the weaving centers set up in France and Spain. Domestic wool was plentiful, being one of the principal sources of much of rural England's wealth, and workshops sprang up in Mortlake, Norwich, and Wilton.

As in France, extensive production only really began in the mid-18th century, and many artists created designs in emulation of their French counterparts. The most important of all these producers was Paresat, who by August 1752 had moved his workshop to Fulham and imported weavers and dyers from France. We know that in 1755, 92 of his weavings in the Savonnerie and Aubusson style were sold at auction.

In the second half of the 18th century, other artists, such as Passavant, Moore, and Thomas Whitty, gained a reputation as accomplished carpet designers and weavers. Whitty (1713-1792) happened to see in the home of a friend several fine examples of imported Turkish carpets, which he set out to reproduce. He established the well-known Axminister workshop, where he produced high quality room-size carpets.

The firm remained in business until 1835, when the looms were bought by Blockmore of the Wilton factory, near Salisbury, which had never before produced hand-knotted carpets (plate 254). Many important carpets woven at Witty's Axminster workshop are well preserved, including neo-classical carpets designed by Robert Adam. The Adam brothers were famous architects and interior designers from Scotland, who designed and commissioned rugs in a rigid classical style that perfectly complemented their buildings (plate 252).

In the 19th century, mechanized processes entered the field of rug weaving – most notably Richard Wystock's invention of chenille weave – and these soon dramatically changed the face of carpet production. This machine-made rug industry boomed in several locations, especially in Scotland.

The aesthetic stagnation brought about by machine technology towards the end of the 19th century spurred John Ruskin and William Morris to demand a return to the traditional methods of rug weaving. Their revolution was both social and aesthetic: an emphasis on good dyes and high-quality craftsmanship characterized Morris's efforts to revive this art. Together with a number of other Victorian artists, Morris popularized the curvilinear floral motifs of the Arts and Crafts movement that became fashionable around the turn of the century. At this time, England made excellent rugs, as well as textiles in a variety of techniques, most notably in art deco and arts and craft period. Virtually no major looms for handmade rugs have been active since World War I, probably because of the high cost of labor.

Other Countries

The prophet of the Arts and Crafts movement in the United States was Gustav Stickley (1858-1942), a furniture maker in Western Massachusetts and upstate New York. He got his ideas of design after he visited France and England, mostly impressed by Voysey and the workshop La Masion de l'Art Noveau. He established his workshop Eastwood, a suburb of Syracuse, NY and in New York City. He made all the furniture himself, but didn't produce any rugs. He still devoted an entire floor of his showroom as a rug gallery. All of the carpets Stickley sold were imported from

plate **238**
AMERICAN HOOKED RUG
20th century
3'7" x 6'3" (1.09 x 1.91m)
The American folk-craft of hooked rugs is one of the richest textile traditions of the USA. These rugs were used for many places in the home but many were hearthrugs. They were made at home and get their name from the technique used of looping the cloth pile through the foundation and leaving a loop, similar to the pile knot but it is left uncut to make pile ends. These are avidly collected in the US, and achieve high prices.

Persia, India, Turkey and Europe and they were all either designed or selected by him (plate 258).

A large industry of carpet making (hooked rugs) developed in America in the late 19th century (plates 238, 260).

Rugs in limited numbers were produced in other European countries, especially after World War II, like Savonnerie style carpets of Austria (plate 243), Czechoslovakia.

The Basarabian Kilims of the 19th century are very different in design and color from the their counterparts in Turkey because adaptation of the influence of French colors and designs (plates 256, 257).

Ukraine, for a while in 19th century, produced some outstanding examples, incorporating French and Russian elements of designs (plate 240).

In Scandinavia, Denmark (plate 239) and Finland (plates 261, 262, 263) made fantastic, minimalist design carpets through the modern period.

plate **239** | Danish Carpet
20th century
7′6″ x 9′8″ (2.29 x 2.95m)
A beautiful Danish carpet of the 20th century with minimalist design resembling folk art of Scandinavia. Like a modern painting on the floor.

European Rugs

plate **240** | Ukrainian Rug
19th century
3′ x 3′ (0.99 x 0.99m)
*This beautiful small rug with an
Ottomanesque floral design
typifies the colors used in the
Ukrainian pile weaving. These
are rare items and were woven
for richest members of society,
many have a royal provenance.*

plate **241** | Spanish Alcaraz
6'10" x 12'5" (2.08 x 3.78m)

This outstanding 16th century carpet was formerly part of Charles Deering's collection. With an allover trelliswork and palmette design and a pallete largely restricted to black and gold this austere and magnificent carpet presents a curious insight into the decorative arts in Renaissance Spain.

The winged creatures, wearing elaborate headgear appear on no other Spanish carpet, although the literature abounds in examples of paired curling dragons similar to those in the border.

The ogival compartments are filled with a crisply drawn, somewhat angular palmette resembling a bishop's miter, carrying as a inner motif a flower with two leaves.

When we look at the multitudes of Renaissance grotesqueries, winged angel heads, and paired curling dragons, we may imagine this carpet influencing the curling dragons and their barbed tongues in the tile borders at the Church of Santo Domingo, Sanlucar de Barrameda, dated 1594.

European Rugs

plate **242** | SAVONNERIE CARPET
Spain
Late 19th/early 20th century
16′5″ x 20′4″ (5.00 x 6.20m)
*The design elements and color in
this example are very French in
appearance, yet the weave
portrays its Spanish origins.
Scrolling pink roses form a band
against an untraditional
chocolate border. The bouquet of
flowers in the center are framed
by two elegantly styled strips of
coupled 'C's. The artwork
mirrors 19th century ceiling
designs of the more elegant
European homes.*

plate **243**
AUSTRIAN SAVONNERIE CARPET
20th century
12′ x 20′6″ (3.66 x 6.25m)
This simple design, similar to tile work, using French porcelain colors, make it desirable for minimalist interiors.

European Rugs

plate **244** | SAVONNERIE
19th century
20′ x 31′6″ (6.10 x 9.60m)
*This particular Napoleon III
period Royal Savonnerie is one
of a few rugs made at the royal
factory still in a private
collection. The rug was formerly
in the palace of King Farouk of
Egypt and is thought to have
been a diplomatic gift from the
French government. The quality
of the design, the surprisingly
fine weaving, and clarity of color
make this a true showpiece for
discerning art lover. The carpet
reflects the taste of the rococo
revival period of carpet weaving
during the middle of the 19th
century, when the decorative
arts flourished in France.*

European Rugs

plate **245** | Savonnerie Carpet
France
Circa 1900
10′4″ x 13′3″ (3.15 x 4.42m)
This carpet has an Art Nouveau design. The traditional design of a large central medallion and flower heads is brought up to date by the creative genius of the Savonnerie workshops.

plate **246** | Aubusson Carpet
France
Late 19th century
9'6" x 13' (2.90 x 3.96m)
*This flatwoven carpet reflects the
simpler and clearer floral and
less architectural and rococo
styles of the early periods of the
19th century. The floriate oval
medallion is repeated in the
corners of the carpet. These
carpets reflect the changes in
taste that French interiors went
through during certain periods.
However there is a continued
architectural theme.*

plate **247** | SAVONNERIE CARPET
France
19th century
11' x 17' (3.35 x 5.18 cm)
The twirling ribbons, floral
swags, and bouquets of roses
give this rug an elegance that is
at home in any environment.

plate **248** | Aubusson Carpet
France
Late 19th century
15′ x 17′7″ (4.57 x 5.36m)
*The coloring of this beautifully
subtle flatwoven carpet reflect
today's taste for soft colors in
carpets. The simple elegance of
the color and design perfectly*
*offset the richly decorated
furniture of the late 19th
century period. These lighter
shades are indicative of the best
of the Aubusson work from the
last quarter of the 19th century
after the revival of the rococo
had subsided.*

plate **249** | Aubusson Carpet
France
Late 18th, early 19th century
15′6″ x 19′ (4.72 x 5.79m)
Graceful lines and soft French blue combined with wonderful gold colors blend beautifully with the exuberant scrolling style of the period.

European Rugs

plate **250** | Aubusson Carpet
19th century
16′ x 17′ (4.88 x 5.18m)
*The color and design elements of
this carpet suggest that it may
have been one of the select
flatwoven carpets ordered for the
redecoration of Versailles.*

plate **251**
ART DECO PERIOD CARPET
France
20th century
8'8" x 13' (2.64 x 3.96m)
*It is not clear where this hand-
knotted carpet was made in
France, but it is clearly part of
the weave of artist designed
carpets and small Ateliers that
became popular in the Art Deco
and modernist period in Paris
and other French cities during
the 1920s and 1930s. These
carpets are keenly collected
today.*

European Rugs

plate **252**
AXMINSTER PALATIAL CARPET
English
19th century
17' x 32' (5.20 x 9.75m)

*This Robert Adam-inspired,
over-all field design creates the
same magnificent composition
and dramatic effect that the
original Regency design would
have had. The scale is large, each
sphere having a circumference of
15" (36 cm). The strength of
colors and immense size suggest
that it was made for a palace or
a palatial residence.*

plate **253** | Savonnerie Carpet
France
Circa 1900
12′6″ x 13′3″ (3.81 x 4.04m)
*An unusually dark palette for a
very full and flowing designed
carpet that echoes the scrolling
vines and medallions of the
earliest Savonnerie production.*

plate **254** | WILTON CARPET
England
Circa 1900
9′9″ x 19′11″ (2.97 x 6.07m)
This carpet dates from the pre-mechanization days of the Wilton carpet factory. This handcrafted carpet combines aspects of Chinese and Turkish carpets with European themes and sensibilities. The medallion has a pair of Fu dogs from the Chinese decorative repertoire, and its circumference is narrowed by the composition of the elements above and below. The main border uses designs from 16th century Turkish rug borders in a very non-Oriental manner since they decorate the field rather than act as a separate border.

European Rugs

plate **256** | Basarabian Kilim
20th century
8'7" x 10' (2.62 x 3.05m)
This art deco design Basarabian Kilim with cream field and soft greens and blues incorporating geometric flowers creates great harmony and beauty.

European Rugs

plate **257** | Basarabian
4′2″ x 6′7″
*Geometric flower and leaf design
shows influence of French and
Turkish ornamentation.*

plate **258** | STICKLEY
(India Drugget Rug)
First quarter of 20th century
6'5" x 8'9" (1.96 x 2.67m)
The prophet of the Arts and Crafts movement in the United States was Gustav Stickley (1858-1942), a furniture maker in western Massachusetts and upstate New York. All of the carpets Stickley sold were imported from Persia, India, Turkey and Europe.
The carpets from India were all a heavy weft-faced plain weave, with several different designs. This example has one of two particularly popular designs. It is an 'India drugget' of type advertised and sold by Stickley 1903-15. The traditional design is woven in Walajapet village, Tamil Nada (formerly Madras) State, southeastern India. It has an Islamic star-and-cross interlace field pattern originally provided to the weavers by Muslim clients in Srinigar, Kashmir, to match their mosaic-inlay wooden ceilings, and a standard Greek-key border used in Indian dhurries. Cotton warp, wool weft. Black on ivory ground.
Similar examples to this rug are illustrated on page 125 of Stickley's 1910 catalogue, on page 53 and 55 of his 1912 catalogue and in the November 1911 issue of his magazine The Craftsman. A more distant variant, with a different but somewhat related pattern can be found at the High Museum of Art, Atlanta, Georgia; Virginia Carroll Crawford Collection. See also plate 362 in Sarah B. Sherrill, Carpets and Rugs of Europe and America, Abbeville Press, 1996.

European Rugs

plate **259**
EUROPEAN ART NOUVEAU CARPET
9′ x 11′ (2.74 x 3.35m)
Evocative of the era, a wonderful
expression of the artistic forces
at work throughout Europe at
the later part of 19th century.

plate **260**
AMERICAN HOOKED RUG
11'7" x 17'6" (3.53 x 5.33m)
*Oval shaped and extra large for
a hooked rug probably is made
to order around the turn of the
century.*

plate **261** | FOLK RUG
Finland
Dated 1939
3′ x 4′8″ (0.91 x 1.42m)

plate **263** | FOLK RUG
Finland
19th century
4′2″ x 5′8″ (1.27 x 1.73m)

plate **262** | FOLK RUG
Finland
Dated 1929
4′8″ x 6′ (1.42 x 1.83m)

European Rugs

Tapestries

Although surviving tapestries, a type of slit weave textile, go as far back as the times of ancient Egypt, for our purpose, most of what is generally referred to as tapestry in our time was developed in the French cities of Arras and Paris in the 14th century. In fact, the name of the town of Arras became synonymous with the word tapestry and is used in different languages to denote tapestry: Arazzi in Italian, Arras in English, Arrasy in Polish, and Paños de Ras in Spanish.

Much has been said about the use of tapestries in medieval times to provide warmth and insulation in the drafty castles of old. Tapestries however, were most importantly, a mobile symbol of status, prestige, and power, and were thus brought out with pride at major events such as weddings, christenings, funerals, baptisms, diplomatic functions, and even carried along to adorn the tents of nobility during military campaigns. Tapestry scholar Guy Delmarcel refers to tapestries as 'the mobile fresco of the North' for the ease with which tapestries could be transported and hung for special occasions, or presented as valuable gifts.

Materials used to weave tapestries are wool and silk, with some highlights in gold and silver threads amongst the more important (and consequently more expensive) sets.

Because they were highly prized in the middle ages, more so than paintings, tapestries were often taken as war booty and susceptible to theft and greed. Also, due to the high cost of materials and long periods it took to produce tapestries, this form of art was normally financed and supported by rich and royal families. There also grew a class of merchant middlemen who would finance the weavers or produce 'on spec' tapestries to be sold in the open market.

For those tapestries that were commissioned, the subjects were often relevant to the sponsors' proclivities, with churches ordering religious subjects, Kings illustrating their military victories, and dreamers and romantics depicting their visions of chivalry and love. Many wealthy land owners commissioned tapestries showing peasants in idyllic life scenes or various modes of play and relaxation, perhaps to ease their guilty consciences over how they treated their subjects.

The Rise of Flemish Tapestry Production

Although tapestry weaving continued in France through the centuries, from the late 15th to the mid 17th century, wars and domestic troubles shifted the bulk of European tapestry production to Flemish towns such as Antwerp, Bruges, Enghien, Oudenaarde, Valenciennes, Ghent, Tournai, and Brussels. The production became most prolific, as trading centers such as Antwerp developed to sell and take orders from patrons who traveled there from all over Europe, and Brussels gained a reputation for making the finest tapestries in the world (plates 268, 269, 270, 271, 272, 275, 276, 277, 279, 280, 281, 282, 283, 285, 290).

The Resurgence of French Tapestry Production

In the 17th century, a concerted effort was made by the French crown to regain its historical dominance in tapestry weaving with the founding of the Royal Gobelins Atelier by Louis XIV in 1662, and the Beauvais factory in 1664 (plates 289, 296).

Although the Beauvais workshop was originally set up as a private factory to produce tapestries for export and non-government commissions. The workshop eventually surpassed in importance all others in the land and truly gained supremacy when Francoise Boucher, whom renowned tapestry expert, George Leland Hunter referred to as 'the greatest tapestry designer of the 18th century,' became resident artist in 1736.

Although there is evidence of tapestry production in Aubusson as far back as the 14th century, production did not gain magnitude until after an edict in 1601 banned the import of foreign (Flemish) 'foliage pieces and verdures.' This was particularly important to Aubusson and the neighboring weaving town of Felletin because their production for the most part consisted of wool on wool scenic tapestries that were quite similar to the famous Flemish verdures of the time. In 1665, the private Aubusson looms were granted an official charter, giving them the status of a royal institution. Although they continued to produce scenic tapestries, in the 18th century the looms of Aubusson fed the popular romanticism with things

plate **265**

FRENCH TAPESTRY PANELS
(SET OF FOUR) – (BEAUVAIS)
THE DORIA PANELS
18th century
2'8" x 12'3" (0.80 x 3.70m)

Each of these two magnificent panels contains grotesques with small birds perched on leaves at the top, a small panel with an ox skull, a vase with a mask above it, flanked by two armless half figures with animal legs, a bull seen head-on, a nude half figure holding up a tray, two dolphin heads, and an armless half figure with wings. In the top and bottom, coats of arms of the Doria family of Genoa are inserted - an eagle with a crown enclosed in a shield. Two flattened scallop shells flank each shield as well as the blank apricot-hued section in the center. Each panel is adorned by garlands and acanthus leaf borders. The 'grotesque', in architecture and decorative art, refers to fanciful mural or sculptural decoration involving mixed animal, human, and plant forms. First revived in the

Renaissance by the school of Raphael in Rome, the grotesque quickly came into fashion in 16th-century Italy and became popular throughout Europe. Although the animal heads and other similar motifs often have heraldic or symbolic significance, grotesque ornaments were, in general, purely decorative. These two pieces are copies of the borders of the 'Neptune' tapestry, from a series of tapestries depicting Olympian Gods surrounded by grotesque borders. The series was woven in the mid-16th century from cartoons after Perino del Vaga, one of Raphael's best-known pupils. The floral border was most likely added to transform the fragments into panels. An illustration of a tapestry from the series, framed within borders identical to these two, can be found in Edith A. Standen, European Post-Medieval Tapestries and Related Hangings in The Metropolitan Museum of Art, Volume I, New York: Metropolitan Museum of Art, 1985.

exotic and 'Chinoiserie.' See plate 287 for an example of a exotic flora tapestry. Notice the royal signature mark on the bottom selvedge.

In the late 19th century, the French, sensing that the tapestry market was no longer the exclusive domain of people with castles and large homes, shifted their production to include smaller, painting size tapestries. Also, color tones were softened to adhere to decorating trends of the period (plates 266, 267, 286, 288, 291, 292, 293).

plate **266**
AUBUSSON TAPESTRY –
FLOWERS AND RIBBONS
19th century
3'9" x 7' (1.14 x 2.13m)
This vertically composed tapestry is an embodiment of the French Rococo style as it was interpreted by the artists of Aubusson. Characteristic elements include a shell and volute cartouche over an oversize tartan bow, scrolling garlands of multicolor blossoms, and life-size floral bouquet, all set within a trumeau-mirror architectural construction.

Identifying Tapestries

The challenges with identifying a particular tapestry are mainly: the narrative, the origin of weave, and time of production.

Many tapestries were woven as sets of four or more episodes in a narrative, with each tapestry telling a part of the story or arranged to showcase a common theme. Very few sets survive in tact, as many perished through the years and others that remained were dispersed through time by heirs of the original owners, sold individually to private owners, re-surfacing only occasionally on their way from one owner to the next. Additionally, most records that could have helped identify the narrative were lost through the centuries.

Another difficulty is that French and Flemish weavers were extremely mobile. Although most of the European tapestries are made in France and Flanders, the fact is that many other countries, such as Spain, Italy, Germany, Austria, Scotland, England, Denmark, Sweden and Poland also produced tapestries. It is however noteworthy that most of these countries imported and naturalized Flemish weavers who had been mas-

plate **267**
AUBUSSON TAPESTRY –
THE FALCONER
19th century
4'3" x 5'2" (1.30 x 1.57m)
A medieval scene updated by scale and colors more practical for the time.

ters of this art for three centuries. Although the actual weaving centers may vary, it can be assumed that Flemish artisans wove most of the tapestries in Europe.

To further complicate matters, most maker's marks and other indications of origin (required in Brussels since 1528, in other parts of Flanders from 1544) were woven in the outer selvedges, the most fragile area of the tapestry.

Borders were almost always ornamental and often had little to do with the main theme of the story depicted in the field. Since tapestry cartoons were re-used by workshops, border design, which often changed according to the fashion senses of the time, are very useful in helping date a tapestry.

English Tapestries

Among the many countries outside of France and Flanders that made tapestries, some of the most outstanding production was in England. Very few dealers or decorators think of English tapestries, and there are many reasons for this. Most often, the tapestries produced in England were commissioned by royalty for particular palaces or abbeys and have remained in these institutions ever since.

The collection of Henry VIII (1471-1530) totaled well over 2000 pieces by the time of his death. English and Scottish Kings were always competing with their French counterparts in supporting royal sponsorship of tapestry workshops and artists. In 1619, King James I appointed Sir Francis Crane to manage and finance the recruitment of Flemish weavers and arranged for their British naturalization.

Crane, with his refined taste and his position as a prominent member of Courts of Elisabeth I, James I and Charles I, started to build a three story building in Mortlake, a few miles Southwest of London. With the help of the King, they recruited Philip de Maecht who worked under de Comans in Paris, and many other artists followed. From 1610 to 1649 some of the most important Mortlake tapestries were made under auspices of the King, with the Prince of Wales and Charles I, the Duke of Buckingham, and other nobles as clients.

American Tapestries

In the 19th and early 20th centuries tapestries increasingly became à la mode for wealthy Americans, and as a consequence, a few tapestry manufactories started production in the nation. The output of these production centers echoed traditional European examples, but gradually transformed into styles and subjects specially suited to American interiors. The changing tastes in interior decoration can be traced through these works of art, and in the 20th century noteworthy modern tapestries proved that this is an art form not only for decorative purposes, but also for expression of ideas and values.

William Baumgarten, one of the most respected design professionals and art connoisseur of his time, founded America's first tapestry workshop in January of 1893. The building boom towards the end of the century had created an increased demand for expensive decorations. Since the wealthy Americans of the time wanted their interiors to resemble that of European royalty of past times, Baumgarten realized the potential of producing fine quality tapestries in the old style in the United States for the affluent clients of his design firm. The main concern of Baumgarten was to match the quality of the antique tapestries so that these new works would be viewed as substitutes of equal value from a technical and artistic point of view. He was fortunate to early on hire away Jean Foussadier and his son Antoine from the Royal Windsor Tapestry Works in England. The Foussadier family had woven tapestries for generations, going back to ateliers in Aubusson and Gobelin. Natural fibers of American manufacture were used. Although different kinds of fibers were employed depending on the design, use, and acceptable cost of each tapestry, white wool or cotton was in most frequent use for the warp, and colored wool or silk and sometimes silver or gold threads for the weft. It was also discovered that the waters of the Bronx river, which flowed by the Atelier's doorstep, had qualities resembling those of the river La Bievre, where the Gobelins first located their dye works in the 15th century. The production of the Baumgarten Atelier, always of great technical merit, improved over the years and came to impress even the French. All Baumgarten tapestries were made with a contract or commission. The Atelier's first commission was for PAB Widener, but soon after, others such as Andrew Carnegie, Charles M. Schwab, and J. Pierpont Morgan, and Jacob H. Schiff followed.

Modern Tapestries

Tapestry as a modern art form, not just reproductions of older scenes came into form in France after the Second World War and inspired other artists across the world to design for tapestry. An interesting example of this type of tapestry can be viewed in plate 297.

During great depression of the 1930's, there was a great art and construction program supported by government, the so called, *WPA*. Many great art works were produced for public buildings. The most important muralists of the time included Mexican born Diego Rivera and Woodstock, New York based artist, Anton Refregier (1905-1979). Both of these artists used funds from the biggest American capitalists to depict the miseries of labor in America at the time.

Anton Refregier's most famous murals are in San Francisco – in the historic Rincon Annex Post Office which is now a museum. In 1960 he started to design tapestries to be woven by Mexican weavers. Setting up this workshop, he was able to produce only four tapestries. One year later, he made a tapestry for Rotron Manufacturing Company. Two tapestries (15 by 21 feet) was made in 1964 for the main office of the Bowery Saving Bank, New York City, and one was created for the Cincinatti airport (plate 295).

Jacquard or 'Hand Loomed' Tapestries

An interesting type of French tapestry, these used a punch card technology and a so called 'Jacquard' loom invented in the 19th century to reproduce popular tapestry motifs in smaller, more affordable versions that were sold during the first three decades of the 20th century (plates 299, 300, 301). Because producing the punch card necessary to make these tapestries was very time and labor intensive, a relatively small number of these were produced. They give a fascinating glimpse into the fashion of the time, with their bold, unapologetic colors, and are quite collectible today.

plate **268**
FLEMISH TAPESTRY (BRUSSELS) –
CEASAR'S TRIUMPHANT RETURN
FROM BATTLE
17th century
11' x 13' (3.35 x 3.96m)

plate **269**
Flemish Tapestry (Oudenaarde)
Mille Fluer
16th century
10′5″ x 15′ (3.18 x 4.57m)
Owing much stylistically to the
15th century blue background so
called Mille Fluer tapestries of
Oudenaarde, the preponderance
of evidence points to our
attribution. In his book, Les
Belles Heures de la Tapisserie
(1978), Dario Boccara illustrates
a tapestry of similar coloring
and field design. He guesses his
tapestry to be German, but in a
later catalogue, changes his
attribution to that of Flanders.

plate **270**

Flemish Tapestry (Brussels)
17th century
11'6" x 14'9" (3.50 x 4.50m)
This tapestry illustrates a turning point in the design and execution of Flemish tapestries. This tapestry is part of the first series created by Pietro Paolo Rubens, and executed at the Brussels workshop of Jan Raes II. Rubens brought his innovative vision to the art of tapestry design by showcasing only a select few monumental figures in his compositions, careful not to clutter the field like his predecessors. This series, depicting the history of the Roman patriot, Decius Mus was probably first commissioned by Sir Dudley Carlton, the Ambassador of his Majesty of Great Britain, to The Hague. The particular scene depicted here is of the presentation of an idol by military leaders to the Roman hero. The Museo de Nacional de Parronico in Spain holds an identical tapestry in their collection.

Tapestries

Tapestries

plate **273**
Aubusson Tapestry –
The Picnic
18th century
7'9" x 13'2" (2.36 x 4.01m)
Since hunting was a universal sport among the leisured nobility, hunting tapestries that combined verdure elements with human figures were always in great demand. In this vibrant example, a classical verdure landscape surrounds a country couple at rest. The lady, in a simple dress and peaked shoes, offers refreshments to her companion, in similar garb. Their baskets are filled to the brim with fruit and other food. A creek floats tranquilly to the right. Behind the seated pair, a hunter and his dog cross the landscape. Two groups of buildings appear in the mid ground. The landscape reaches into the distant hills, offering the viewer a magnificent panorama.

plate **274**
Paris Tapestry –
Zeus Seducing Diana
17th century
10'7" x 12'8" (3.23 x 3.86m)
Zeus, assuming another of his protean transformations, attempts the seduction of Diana, Goddess of the Hunt, in a lush leafy flower strewn bower. While he assumes the disguise of a young maiden, he is accompanied by his heraldic symbol of the eagle. Diana reclines in her warrior antique garb, complete with a quiver of arrows. Using the popular convention the multiple episode and image, in the skies of the distant background, Hermes (Mercury), the messenger god, points towards the approaching twilight. On four sides of this image, highly detailed lavish floral and foliate columns are centered with elaborate shields and augmented with fruit and vegetable filled baskets.

plate **275**

Flemish Tapestry (Brussels) –
Suleiman Marries the Emperor
Emmanuel's Niece
17th century
12' x 12'4" (3.62 x 3.76m)
*The vividly depicted scene is from
the epic of the legendary Mongol
conqueror Tamerlaine, victor over
the Turkish Sultan Bajazet I, at
Angora in 1402. In the 17th
century, the military might of the
Ottoman empire was especially
feared throughout Europe, thus
the popularity of depictions of
defeats of this Oriental foe,
whose power was decisively
broken following the raising of
the siege of Vienna in 1683.
In this episode, which
commemorates the victory of
Tamerlaine's armies of the West
over Sultan Bajazet I's conquered
forces of the East, Suleiman,
Bajazet's son, is wed to the niece
of Emmanuel, Emperor of
Constantinople. For the 17th
century viewer, it illustrated the
triumph of a well-known earlier
battle while celebrating the
contemporary success of Western
forces. A tapestry of this identical
scene, with a different border is in
the Kunsthistorisches Museum,
Vienna.*

*This exceptionally fine example
of a well-loved genre – the
Flemish verdure tapestry – is a
carefully composed landscape.
The eyes of the viewer focus on
lush white flowers in front of
dense foliage and pause on a life
size water bird. A stream divides
the landscape, leading the viewer
to a group of buildings in the
distance. A lavish fruit and
foliate garland, with two repeats
of the central water bird image
frame this well-balanced image.*

plate **277**

FLEMISH TAPESTRY (BRUSSELS)
ZEUS AND HERA
17th century
10'8" x 13'3" (4.09 x 3.24m)

Zeus is the mighty bearded man seated on his throne with an eagle holding a thunderbolt at his right shoulder, Hera holding a scepter, and Eros is shown lifting a globe. The entire composition is framed within elaborate floral and foliate architectural borders composed of garland and cherubs, with a caryatid holding a cornucopia, a satyr in the shape of Dionysus pouring wine from an ewer. Zeus (whose Roman name is Jupiter) is the Ruler of Heaven and Earth, of all other gods, and of all men. The Greeks respected him for his protection of the weak, his justice, wisdom and power. They also understood his passions and infidelities, which rendered him more human and easier to understand. Zeus is a god of light and sky, and his attribute is the lightning bolt. The eagle is both his symbol and his messenger. One of the eight wives of Zeus is Hera (Juno is her Roman name). She is the Queen of gods, the Goddess of Marriage and Maternity, and represents the idealized wife. Hera is a figure of majesty, wearing a diadem on her head. Her attributes are a scepter surmounted by a cuckoo, the pomegranate and the peacock. Eros (Cupid) is the God of Love, a small, winged boy, carrying bow and arrows. His arrows pierce the heart, causing the victim fall in love. Eros is the youngest of all gods, and some traditions relate that he was born from a silver egg. His Roman name Cupid is derived from the Latin cupido, meaning 'desire'.

Tapestries

plate **278**
<small>FRENCH TAPESTRY (AUBUSSON)</small>
18th century
8'4" x 15'8" (2.54 x 4.78m)
*A more sophisticated drawing
than its Flemish counterparts,
this French Verdure shows a
willingness to add to the color
pallete.*

Tapestries

plate **279**
FLEMISH TAPESTRY (OUDENAARDE)
THE CROWNING
16th century
8′ x 10′9″ (2.47 cm x 3.27m)
*A dramatic episode of courtly
life, with a life-size bearded king
in antique dress crowning an
enthroned queen – both being
viewed by a group of highly
individualized full-length male
and female figures. The visual
composition, and the strongly
allegorical nature of the male
and female participants along
with their dress and symbolic
attributes suggests that this
vignette is part of a larger series
of didactic events in either an
historical or mythological
legend. On all four sides, a lush
meandering garland of floral
and foliate swags is augmented
with antique urns.*

Tapestries

plate **280**
Flemish Tapestry (Brussels) –
The Coronation
17th century
8′7″ x 12′2″ (2.62 x 3.71m)
*Possibly depicting the crowning
of Flavia Maxima Fausta, wife of
the great Emperor Constantine.*

plate **281**
FLEMISH TAPESTRY (BRUSSELS) –
DIDO BURNS THE ARMOR
OF ANEAS
17th century
9'3" x 12'4" (2.82 x 3.76m)
Aeneas and his band of warriors,
much like Odysseus, wandered
the seas following the Trojan
War. He happened upon and
island where Dido, Queen of the
Phoenicians, had exiled herself
to, and decides to marry her and
settle down in his new kingdom.
The love story is interrupted
however, when Hermes, the
messenger god is dispatched by
Zeus to urge Aeneas to continue
his journey toward Hesperia
(now Italy).
Distraught over the impending
departure of Aeneas, Dido begs
him to reconsider, and then
burns his armor. Aeneas leaves
anyway, and the distraught Dido
considers killing herself.

Tapestries

plate **282**
FLEMISH TAPESTRY (BRUSSELS)
TELEMACHUS THROWN INTO THE
SEA, FROM THE ADVENTURES OF
TELEMACHUS SERIES
18th century
9′ x 11′10″ (2.74 x 3.61m)
After the shipwreck of his boat,
Telemachus (the son of Ulysses
and Peneloppe) spend some time
on the island of Calypso and fell
in love with Eucharis, one's of
Calypso's nymphs. Cupid, the
god of Love, incited the other
nymphs to burn the new boat in
order to delay Telemachus
departure and they did. But
Mentor, his guardian (in fact
Minerva disguised as an old
man) wanted him to leave the
island and come back to Itaca so
he pushed Telemachus into the
sea where they were picked up
by a passing vessel.
Inspired by novel of Fenelon
published in 1699 - this scene is
not depicted in Homer's the
Odyssey. Signature of
the weaver V. Leyniers
(for Urbain Leyniers,
active between 1720 and 1729)
Designed by Jean van Orley
(1665 - 1735)

plate **283**
FLEMISH TAPESTRY –
SERENE SCENE
18th century
8′6″ x 10′ (2.60 x 3.05m)
This excellent example of
Flemish verdure tapestry
combines the classical
components of this genre. Lush
trees in the foreground guide the
eyes of the viewer to the white
flowers in front and pause on
two life size water birds.
An exquisite lavish floral border
frames this well-balanced
composition.

Tapestries

plate **284**
FRENCH TAPESTRY (AUBUSSON –
CHASING BIRDS
18th century
9'4" x 10'4" (2.84 x 3.15m)
*A delightful vignette of the
bucolic pleasures of country life.
The central focus is a playful
genre scene – three country folk
(two women and one man)
chasing local wild birds.*

plate **285**
FLEMISH TAPESTRY (BRUSSELS) –
THE CROWN OF VICTORY
6′ x 8′ (1.83 x 2.44m)
*In this dramatic tapestry the
chronicles of war are illustrated.
Extraordinarily rich in detail
and swarming with figures and
battlements, this tapestry gives
the viewer a remarkably
accurate impression of ancient
combat. Beginning at the upper
left corner the battle episodes
evolve before the eyes of the
viewer - the preparation and
distribution of arms, the troops
gathering before the attack.
Crossing over to the upper right
corner, the invasion of the city is
portrayed and a tumultuous
battle takes place. Recalling the
pictorial devices of
Netherlandish painting, these
battle vignettes, while in the
distance, are of incredible detail
and accuracy. The warriors
gather and weapons are
surrendered to the winners. In
the center foreground, the
standing ruler is paid homage to
by his kneeling soldier, both
individuals vividly portrayed in
life size, standing amongst the
trophies and spoils of war,
including the crowns of victory.
The victorious soldier wears a
fold-over 'Phrygian cap', an
ancient symbol of liberty.*

plate **286**
FRENCH TAPESTRY (AUBUSSON) –
COUNTRY LIFE
19th century
6'7" x 9'6" (2.00 x 2.90m)
*This exquisitely fine quality
tapestry is an elegant expression
of French artistry relating to a
bucolic farm scene. The
composition gives us an
idealized glimpse into country
life. A woman feeds the hens
with seeds from her apron while
a man seated on a wheelbarrow
overlooks. The costume details
are meticulously rendered. This
carefully depicted country scene
includes a river and a farmhouse
on a hill. The heraldic shield
centered on the upper frame,
while unidentified at present
suggests that this part of a
commission series.*

Tapestries

plate **287**
Aubusson Tapestry –
Exotic Flora
18th century
8' x 13' (2.44 x 3.96m)
Exotic architecture is combined with flora and fauna in a classically structured composition. A life-size coconut tree, palm tree and abundant flower plants frame a turkey hen and cock and a flying macaw in front of a slender triple column garden pavilion. In the distance, *beyond a wide river, a jungle landscape overlooks broad waterfalls. A stepped mountainous road leads to a temple rising above lush forest. The design elements of this remarkable scene suggest that this fantasy landscape is an imaginary view of the New World. The signature indicates that this tapestry was woven after the Aubusson workshops received royal accreditation.*

390

plate **288**

FRENCH TAPESTRY (AUBUSSON)
19th century
8'9" x 9'9" (2.70 x 3.00m)
*In the center foreground of this
splendid tapestry, a bird of prey
has landed on a branch. A river
divides the scenery and leads the
eyes of the viewer from the lush
floral and foliate foreground
through the landscape towards a
lake and a village in the
distance.*

plate **289**
FRENCH TAPESTRY (BEAUVAIS) –
THE GODDESS FLORA
AND HER MAIDS
18th century
11′x 11′3″ (3.35 x 3.43m)
This particularly fine example of
the works of the Beauvais atelier
illustrates Flora (Chloris in
Greek mythology), the goddess
of blossoming flowers, and the
personification of Spring. This
tapestry is part of a series of
seven pieces called 'The Triumph
of the Gods'.

plate **290**
FLEMISH TAPESTRY –
THE TRIUMPH OF TRUTH, JUSTICE,
AND PERSEVERANCE OVER LUST
AND ENVY
17th century
9′ x 9′8″ (2.74 x 2.95m)
*Full of symbolism, the coat of
arms is that of the Count of
Monterrey, who was the
governor of the Spanish
Netherlands from 1670 to 1675.
The tapestry was probably
commissioned by the 8th
Marquis de la Lapilla, Duque de
Centurion in Maples.*
*(Source: Elenco de Garndezas,
Titulos Nobiliaris del Reino,
Madrid 1998)*
*The cross, back of the coat of
arms is the insignia of the order
of Santiago. The Duke was
knight of the Order of Santiago.
1st quarter of main coat of arms
is the Fonseca family.*

*This joyful, extremely fine
Rococo revival tapestry depicts a
courting couple and a young
maiden, seated next to a gently
flowing stream, all in a bucolic
landscape. The couple exchange
love gifts and floral wreaths, the
young maiden with her devoted
pet dog illustrates to the viewer
the promise of fidelity ('Fido')
that accompanies romantic love.
The asymmetry of the
composition, the lush floral and
foliate embellishments and
ghostly pagoda in the far
distance herald the arrival of the
Romantic period in the
decorative arts. The light and
lucid impression is derived from
the French fascination with
portraying serene nature in
colors that coordinate perfectly
with their meticulously
decorated interiors. Although the
tapestry is most luminous, the
carefully rendered details are
highly visible, bearing witness of
the masterful skill of the maker.*

Tapestries

plate **294**

FRENCH TAPESTRY (AUBUSSON)
Early 19th century
8'5" x 13'3" (2.57 x 4.04m)
*This ravishing tapestry
illustrates a number of carefully
depicted themes. In the
foreground a dog hunts a pair of
ducks, a peacock sits on top of a
lavish ornamental fountain. A
magnificent chateau and a
formal garden surrounded by a
moat stand before a distant
snowy mountainous landscape.*

*Exotic botanical elements
frame this classically balanced
composition. They include on the
left a grapevine, on the right a
fruit tree, along with blossom
plants.*

plate **295**
MODERN TAPESTRY BY ANTON
REFREGIER
Mid 20th century
9′ x 29′ (2.72 x 8.85m)
This tapestry depicts work scenes
that were a typical subject of
Refregier's murals and was
probably commissioned for the
airport in Cincinnati, Ohio.

plate **296**
BEAUVAIS SILK AND METAL
TAPESTRY – BOUCHER'S ROSES
18th century
10′6″ x 4′ (3.20 x 1.22m)
Eight exquisite bouquets of pale
roses decorate these rare leaf
green striped silk and metallic
woven panels.

plate **297**
FRENCH 'MODERNIST TAPESTRY'
4'8" x 6' (1.42 x 1.83m)
*Signed by Herve' Lelong, a great
example of mid 20th century
revival of innovative tapestry
design.*

Tapestries

plate **298**
FRENCH TAPESTRY (AUBUSSON) –
CROSSING OF THE GRANIQUE
17th century
9'4" x 12' (2.84 x 3.66m)
*From the 'History of Alexander
the Great' series, it was woven
based on a the paintings of Le
Brun. The tapestry does have the
royal signature, and is one of
many made from this scene. One
version is in The Museo
Nacional de Arte Antigua in
Portugal.*

Tapestries

plate **299**
HAND LOOMED TAPESTRY
(FRANCE)
20th century
6'3" x 8'2" (1.91 x 2.49m)
Interesting that such a quintessentially English scene was chosen for this French Jacquard

plate **300**
HAND LOOMED TAPESTRY
(FRANCE)
20th century
4'5" x 5' (1.35 x 1.52m)
Notice the red wallpaper sky in this brilliantly colorful scene.

plate **301**
HAND LOOMED TAPESTRY
(FRANCE)
5' x 7' (1.52 x 2.13m)
The romantic genre scene framed elaborately

Bibliography

Adelson, CJ, *European Tapestry*, The Minneapolis Institute of Art, 1994

Alexander, Christopher, *A Foreshadowing of 21st century Art: The Color And Geometry Of Early Turkish Carpets*, Oxford University Press, 1993

Benardout, R, *Caucasian Rugs*, Reymond Benardout, England, 1978

Bennett, I, *Jail Birds*, An Exhibition of 19th Century Indian Carpets, 1987

Berinstain, V, Day, S, Floret, E, Galea-Blanc, C, Gelle, O, Mathias, M, Ziai, A, *Great Carpets of the World*, Thames and Hudson, London, 1996

Blazkova, J, *Wandteppiche*, Artia Prag, 1957

Black, D, Loveless, C, *The Undiscovered Kilim*, London, 1977

Böde, W, *Vorderasiatische Knüpfteppiche*, Verlag von Hermarn Seemaun Nachfolger, Leipzig, n.d.
Altorientalische Tierteppiche, Vienna, 1892

Bogolyubov, AA, edited by Thompson, J, *Carpets of Central Asia*, Crosby Press, 1973

Bidder, H, *Carpets from East Turkestan*, Tubingen, 1964

Bocchara, D, *Les Belles Heures de la Tapisserie*, 1978

Boralevi, A, *Sumakh - Flat-woven carpets of the Caucasus*, Karta, Firenze, 1986

Breck, J, & Morris, F, *The Ballard Collection of Oriental Rugs*, New York, 1923

Bruggemann, W, and Bohmer, H, *Rugs of the Peasants and Nomads of Anatolia*, Kunst und Antiquitäten, Munich, 1983

De Calatchi, R, *Oriental Carpets*, Charles F. Tuttle Company, Rutland, Vermont, 1967

Calvert, AF, *The Spanish Royal Tapestries*, John Lane Company, New York

Candee, HC, *The Tapestry Book*, Tudor Publishing Co., New York, 1935

Cavallo, AS, *Medieval Tapestries*, The Metropolitan Museum of Art, New York, 1993

Chevalier, D, Chevalier, P, Bertrand, P, *Les tapisseries d'Aubusson et de Felletin*, Solange Thierry Editeur, Paris, 1988

Clark, H, *Bokhara, Turkoman and Afghan Rugs*, John Lane and Bodley Head Ltd., London, 1922

Coen, L & Duncan, L, *The Oriental Rug*, Harper and Row, New York, 1978

Coffinet, J. *L'Art de la Tapisserie*, Imprimerie Studer, Geneve, 1971

Cohen, S, *The Unappreciated Dhurrie*, London, 1982

David, CB, *French Tapestries & Textiles*, The J. Paul Getty Museum, Los Angeles, 1997

Delmarcel, G, *Flemish Tapestry*, Abrams, Harry N. Incorporated, 2000

Delmarcel, G, *Flemish Tapestries - Five Centuries of Tradition*, Vianden Castle, Luxemburg, 1995

Delmarcel, G, *Golden weavings - Flemish Tapestries of the Spanish Crown*, The Gaspard De Wit Foundation, Malines, 1993

Dilley, AU, *Oriental Rugs and Carpets*, (revised edition), M.S. Dimand, Lippincott, New York, 1959

Edwards, AC *The Persian Carpet*, Duckworth, London, 1953

Eiland, Murray L Jr, & Eiland III, Murray, *Oriental Rugs: A Complete Guide*, Calman & King Ltd, 1998

Eiland, Murray L Jr, *Oriental Rugs from Pacific Collections*, San Francisco Bay Area Rug Society, San Francisco, 1990

Ellis, CG, *Oriental Carpets in the Philadelphia Museum of Art*, Philadelphia Museum of Art, 1998

Ellis, CG, *Early Caucasian Rugs*, The Textile Museum, Washington, DC, 1976

Ellwanger, WD, *The Oriental Rug*, Dodd, Mead & Company, New York, 1903

Erdmann, K, *700 Years of Oriental Carpets*, Berkeley, University of California Press, 1970

Emery, I, *The Primary Structure of Fabrics*, The Textile Museum, Washington, DC, 1966

Fogg Catalogue, foreword by Joseph V McMullan; introduction and notes by Christopher Dunham Reed, Cambridge, Massachusetts, Harvard University, William Hayes Fogg Art Museum, 1966

Ford, JPJ, *The Oriental Carpet, History and Guide to Motifs, Patterns and Symbols*, Thames and Hudson, New York 1992

Franses, J, *European and Oriental Rugs for Pleasure and Investment*, Arco, New York, 1970

Franses, J, *Tapestries and their Mythology*, John Gifford, London, 1973

Gans-Ruedin, E, *Antique Oriental Carpets*, Kodansha International, Tokyo, 1975

Gans-Ruedin, F, *Indian Carpets*, Rizzoli International Publications Inc, 1984

Gans-Ruedin, F, *Caucasian Carpets*, Rizzoli International Publications Inc, 1986

Gantzhorn, V, *Oriental Carpets*, Taschen, Köln, 1998

Ghazarian, M, *Armenian Carpet*, Editions Erebouni, 1988

Göbel, H *Wandteppiche*, Verlag von Klinkhardt & Biermann, Leipzig, 1923

Hackmack, A, *Chinese Carpets and Rugs*, translated by L Arnold, Tientsin-Peking, La Librairie Française Tientsin, Pejyang Press, 1924

Harrow L, Franses J, *The Riverbank Collection - Silk Rugs from Turkey and Persia*, Scorpion Cavendish, London, 1996

Hasson, R, *Caucasian Rugs*, L.A. Mayer Memorial Institute for Islamic Art, Jerusalim, 1986

Hawley, W, *Oriental Rugs*, Dodd, Mead and Co, New York, 1922

Holt, RB, *Rugs, Oriental and Occidental*, Garden City Publishing Company Garden City, New York, 1937

Herrmann, E, *Seltene Orientteppiche*, Volume I-X, Munich, 1978-1988

Hubel, RG, *The Book of Carpets*, Praeger, New York, 1970

Hunter, GL, *The Practical Book of Tapestries*, J.B. Lippincott Company, Philadelphia, 1925

Iten-Maritz, J, *Turkish Carpets*, Kodansha International, Tokyo, 1977

Izmidlian, G, *Oriental Rugs and Carpets Today*, Hippocrene Books, New York, 1977

Jacobsen, C, *Check Points on How to Buy Oriental Rugs*, Charles F. Tuttle, Rutland, Vermont, 1967

Jarry, Madeleine, *World Tapestry*, G.P. Putnam's Sons, New York, 1968

Kazak del XIX Secolo, Moshe Tabibnia, Milano, 1995

Kendrick, AF and Tattersall CEC, *Hand-Woven Carpets: Oriental and European*, New York, 1973

Kerimov, L, *Azerbaijan Carpets*. Baku, 1961

Kirchheim, H, *Orient Stars*, Stuttgart and London, 1993

Landreau, A, and Pickering, W, *From the Bosporous to Samarkand, Flat-Woven Rugs*, The Textile Museum, Washington, DC, 1969

Lewis, G, *Practical Book of Oriental Rugs*, Lippincoff, Philadelphia, 1911

Loges, W, *Turkmenische Teppiche*, Bruckniann Munchen, 1978

Lorentz, HA, *A View of Chinese Rugs from the Seventeenth to the Twentieth Century*. Routledge and Kegan Paul, London, 1973

Mackie, LW and Thompson, J, *Turkmen - Tribal Carpets and Traditions*, The Textile Museum, Washington DC, 1980

Morehouse, B, *Yastiks*, Philadelphia, 1996

Moshkova, VG, *Carpets of the People of Central Asia*, ed. by O'Bannon, GW, Tuscon, 1996

McMullan, J, and Reichert, D, *The George Walter Vincent and Belle Townsley Smith Collection of Islamic Rugs*, George Walter Vincent Smith Art Museum, Massachusetts, n.d.

Mumford, JK, *Oriental Rugs*, Scribners, New York, 1900

O'Bannon, G, *The Turkoman Carpet*, Gerald Duckworth and Co., London, 1974

Opie, J, *Trabal Rugs*, Portland, 1981

Ortiz, AD, Carretero, CH, Godoy, JA, *Resplendence of the Spanish Monarchy*, The Metropolitan Museum of Art, New York, 1991

Petsopoulos, Y, *Kilims - Masterpieces form Turkey*, Rizzoli International Publications, New York, 1991

Phillips, B, *Tapestry*, Phaidon Press Ltd, London, 1994

Pope, AU, *A Survey of Persian Art*, London, 1938-39

Raphaelian, H, *Rugs of Armenia*. An Anatol Sivas Publication, New York, 1960

Reed, S, *Oriental Rugs and Carpets*, Putnam, New York, 1967

Saunders, PE, *Tribal Visions*, Marin Cultural Center, Navao, 1981

Schürmann, U, *Caucasian Rugs*, The Crosby Press, Basingstoke, 1974

Schürmann, U, *Central Asian Rugs*, Verlag Osterneth, Frankfurt, 1969

Sehuyler, F, *Turkistan*, Scribner, Armstrong & Co, New York, 1877

Sherrill, SB, *Carpets and Rugs of Europe and America*, Abbeville Press, New York, 1993

Spuhler, F, *Islamic Carpets and Textiles in the Keir Collection*, Faber and Faber, 1978

Standen, FA, *European Post-Medieval Tapestries*, The Metropolitan Museum of Art, New York, 1985

Straka, J, *The Oriental Rug Collection*, Jerome A. Straka, New York, 1978

Thacher, AB, *Turkoman Rugs*. F Weyne, New York, 1940

The Tiffany Studios, *Antique Chinese Rugs*, Charles E. Tuttle Company, Rutland, Vermont, 1970

Thomson, WG, *A History of Tapestry*, Hodder and Stoughton London, 1906

Thomson, F.P, *Tapestry - Mirror of History*, Crown Publishers, Inc., New York, 1980

Tschebull, R, *Kazak*. Introduction by Joseph V Mc Mullan, Near Eastern Art Research Center, New York Rug Society, 1971

Turkoman Rugs, foreword by Joseph V McMullan; introduction and notes by Cristopher Dunham Reed, Harvard University, William Hayes Fogg Art Museum, Cambridge, Massachusetts, 1966.

Verlet, P, Florisoone, M, Hoffmeister, A, Tabard, F, *The Book of Tapestry - History and Technique*, The Vendome Press, Lausanne, 1978

Victoria and Albert Museum Guide to the Collections of Carpets, London, 1931

Weeks, J, and Treganowan, D, *Rugs and Carpets of Europe and the Western World*. Weathervane Books, New York, 1969

Welch, SA, *King's Book of Kings*, New York Graphic Society, Connecticut, 1972

A special thank you to the photographers
whose work appears in this book.

Hossein Montazaran, Carpet Photo

Plates: 2, 3, 4, 5, 6, 7, 10, 11, 13, 14, 15, 17, 18, 19, 21, 24, 25, 27, 29, 32, 33, 34, 35, 38, 39, 40, 42, 43, 45, 46, 47, 48, 49, 50, 51, 52, 53, 54, 55, 57, 60, 61, 62, 63, 64, 65, 66, 70, 71, 72, 73, 74, 75, 76, 77, 78, 79, 80, 81, 82, 84, 85, 86, 87, 88, 89, 90, 91, 92, 94, 96, 97, 98, 100, 101, 103, 104, 105, 109, 111, 113, 114, 115, 117, 118, 121, 122, 123, 124, 125, 128, 129, 130, 132, 133, 134, 135, 136, 137, 138, 139, 140, 142, 143, 144, 145, 146, 147, 148, 149, 150, 151, 152, 153, 154, 155, 156, 158, 160, 161, 162, 164, 165, 167, 168, 170, 171, 173, 174, 175, 176, 178, 179, 180, 181, 182, 183, 184, 185, 187, 188, 190, 191, 192, 193, 194, 195, 196, 200, 201, 202, 203, 204, 205, 206, 208, 209, 210, 211, 212, 213, 215, 216, 217, 219, 220, 221, 222, 223, 224, 225, 226, 228, 229, 230, 231, 233, 234, 235, 236, 239, 240, 241, 243, 245, 247, 250, 253, 256, 257, 258, 259, 261, 262, 264, 265, 266, 267, 268, 270, 271, 272, 273, 275, 276, 278, 279, 280, 281, 282, 283, 284, 285, 287, 288, 289, 290, 291, 292, 293, 294, 296, 297, 298, 299, 300, 301

John Bigelow Taylor

Plates: 22, 36, 56, 58, 68, 83, 232, 242, 246, 254, 255, 295

Don Tuttle

Plates: 8, 9, 20, 23, 26, 28, 30, 31, 41, 59, 67, 69, 93, 95, 106, 116, 119, 120, 126, 127, 141, 157, 159, 169, 197, 198, 199, 207, 218, 227, 238, 244, 248, 249, 252, 269